Daniel Bedinger Lucas, William Alexander MacCorkle, James Fairfax McLaughlin

Nicaragua

War of the filibusters

Daniel Bedinger Lucas, William Alexander MacCorkle, James Fairfax McLaughlin

Nicaragua
War of the filibusters

ISBN/EAN: 9783743309258

Manufactured in Europe, USA, Canada, Australia, Japa

Cover: Foto ©ninafisch / pixelio.de

Manufactured and distributed by brebook publishing software (www.brebook.com)

Daniel Bedinger Lucas, William Alexander MacCorkle, James Fairfax McLaughlin

Nicaragua

INTRODUCTORY.

At five o'clock on the morning of May 1st of this year, I was awakened, in San José, Costa Rica, by the firing of cannon and the noise of a brass band parading the streets. On picking up the morning papers I learned that the demonstration was an act of rejoicing over the surrender in Nicaragua of "el filibustéro Yankee William Walker," on the 1st of May, 1857—thirty-eight years ago. With my coffee I glanced over that morning's issue of six of the eight daily papers of the city, and each one contained an editorial glorification of the heroic action of the Central Americans in expelling Walker and his followers from their soil. These articles were pitched on a high and patriotic key; and some of the papers denounced in manly terms all species of interference in the Home Rule of these countries by outsiders.

On the evening of the same day, a distinguished local orator delivered an address in Congress Hall before an interested audience of the representative, ruling citizens of Costa Rica, having the Walker invasion as his theme.

My attention having thus been drawn to the general subject, I found, on looking around, many evidences in Costa Rica of the lively interest still felt in the effort of William Walker to subjugate Nicaragua, with a view of planting therein another race of people.

I also remembered that in Nicaragua, the 14th of September, the anniversary of the defeat of Walker's forces at San Jacinto in 1856, in which skirmish Byron Cole lost his life, is annually celebrated; and that in March of last year, the present Liberal Government of Nicaragua disinterred the bones of General Maxímo Jérez, which had been smouldering in the church-yard at Rivas, and with much pomp of parade, carried them across the Republic, exhibiting them in state at Granada and Managua, and depositing then in a vault at Leon.*

These ceremonies, which extended over more than one week, were given all the significance which public speeches, flags and banners, parades and music, cannon and skyrockets could bestow. The day upon which General Ortiz would arrive at Leon with his troops fresh from their victorious campaign in expelling the Conservative President Vesquez from Honduras and installing Dr. Policarpo Bonilla, a Liberal, in his stead, was selected as that upon which

---

* Leon had been adopted by the Directory of the Liberal Revolutionists of 1854, as their capital of Nicaragua; while tho Legitimate government, whose President was Fruto Chamorro, continued to administer its authority at Granada. Cole, who was killed at San Jacinto, was the American with whom the Liberal Directory made the first contract to bring immigrants, with the guaranteed right to bear arms, into Nicaragua; and this was the invitation which Walker accepted.

the climax of the celebration was to take place. The country people and the soldiery of the Republic overran the quaint old city which had been a seat of many a destructive quake, both of the earth and of political factions.

I have thus briefly pointed to some of the evidence that, after the lapse of nearly forty years, the Walker invasion is a reality with the people of Costa Rica and Nicaragua. The generation which knew Walker has, with Walker himself, passed over the Divide, but the patriotic spirit which repelled his intrusion is as bright in this generation as it was in 1856-'7. At that time there were a few intelligent citizens who believed at first that the United States Government, under the influence of the slaveholding element then dominant at Washington, was either openly backing Walker or giving him its covert encouragement, and Walker shrewdly disseminated that idea—apparently believing it himself. Some of these people hoped that this incursion of filibusters would result in the incorporation of these countries as a part of the Great Republic of the North. There are even now a few good citizens, natives, who would be pleased to see annexation and who could be induced to occupy seats in the Senate and in the House of Representatives at Washington from the States of Nicaragua and Costa Rica, but they are intelligent enough to understand that there is but little desire on the part of the people of the United States for the annexation of a foot of territory lying south of that country.

They appreciate the impolicy of the Great Republic bringing into its political system a territory peopled almost exclusively by another race, who speak another language, profess a different religion, who are accustomed to a code of laws foreign to our jurisprudence, whose modes of thought and social habits are widely dissimilar from ours, and who, while aspiring to the advantages of Republican institutions, are, by all of the above reasons, not yet prepared to enter the family of the Federal States. These men well understand that, while all Americans have a keen sympathy with any people who may be struggling for independence from a tyrannical foreign master, they are not reaching out for the annexation of such people. Uncle Sam prefers to have them as friendly neighbors rather than as members of his own household. There is no longer any delusion among the intelligent people of Central America upon this point.

It was in Leon that the revolution of July, 1893, in Nicaragua, was organized and carried to a successful conclusion, by which the Conservative Administration of President Machado was driven out and the Liberal Administration of President Zelaya was brought into power. General Zelaya, who had been one of the bravest and most skillful leaders of the Conservative revolt in the preceding April, now cast his fortunes with the Liberal up-rising and led the Leon forces to victory. In this manner was inaugurated the first administration pledged to the principles of the Liberal party since the days of Walker.

The fact that the Liberal leaders of 1854 invited Walker to come to their aid against the Granada (Conservative) government and that they afterwards joined the latter, and even invited aid from the sister Republics, in expelling the armed immigrants from their soil, will not appear in an inconsistent light when a clear view is had of the whole situation.

When the Liberal leaders contracted with Walker and his associates, they had only in mind the idea of utilizing the Americans in acquiring political power for themselves at the expense of the Conservative faction. The Americans were hired with salaries and lands for this purpose only. They were to fight as the Hessians fought for Great Britain in the American revolution—as mere mercenaries. They were to fight in a cause which appealed to no sentiment of patriotism, to kill people with whom they had no quarrel. They were to have no social position in the community; no position except that of hired butchers of one faction of natives in order that another faction might hold the reins of government. With this understanding of the mission of the American immigrants, the latter were given a genuinely hearty welcome by the Liberals. The dignitaries of the Provisional government and of Leon, which city was at that time the second in size and importance in Central America, went out to meet them with cordial greetings. On their arrival, the streets overflowed with crowds of people who vied with each other in demonstrations of good will toward their American deliverers. A great feast was spread, and sympathetic women, with beaming faces, sparkling eyes, arrayed in the attractive soft colors worn by the sex in the tropics, thronged around them and poured forth most grateful thanks for the protection promised them, their children and their homes, from their Granada rulers. These simple hearted people meant it all. They were sincere in their exhibition of good will. But their enthusiasm rested upon a misapprehension.

Notwithstanding, Walker and his men were to receive moneyed salaries and lands from the Liberals for their military services, they had no intention of fighting the battles of one native faction against another faction of natives. They did not come to raise up the down trodden, nor to defend the weak against their oppressors. Walker came to prosecute a war, having quite a different object. He came in the character of a conqueror. His mission was to overthrow the then existing social conditions and to reconstruct the industrial system. He was a believer in an irrepressible conflict between races; a believer in the theory of a survival of the fittest. He came to plant a colony of Anglo-Saxon civilization; and he recognized that this could only be done over the graves of the mixed races which then occupied the country. He took early steps for the transfer of the lands to the conquerors, for he reasoned rightly that only by the possession of the soil could the conquerors hold permanent control. His object was to "regenerate" the country, as he called it, by the establishment of a labor system which would secure the highest cultivation of the rich soil, and coin the valuable forests and mines into gold. Being a son of a slave-holding State, he proposed to erect his social, political, and industrial fabric with African slavery as its corner-stone.

Walker's eye had not caught even a glimpse of the first rays of the new day of universal freedom throughout all the Americas, which was about to dawn. He had no prophetic vision which enabled him to see that within ten years from that time the foot of no black slave would press the soil of the United States, and that within the life of a generation liberty to the African would prevail from Alaska to Patagonia.

But it is not a matter of wonder that this fair land, lying waste for the want of a stable government and a reliable labor system, should strongly attract a talented, ambitious, resolute, restless man. That such a man, who was at the same time a devout believer in the beneficence of the institution of negro slavery to both the white and black races, should have coveted this field for an exhibition of his prowess, the exercise of his statemanship, and the introduction of a system of labor to which he was attached, is not surprising.

Walker found here a country as picturesque in its mountains, plains, and lakes ; as rich in its productions ; as equable in temperature ; as salubrious in climate in most of its area as was ever created for the use of man ; a country whose soil is as fecund as the banks of the Nile, whose rains are as fertilizing as the dews of Egypt, whose sunshine is as fructifying as the heat of a conservatory ; a country where frosts never come to chill the tender fruits, nor burning heats to blast the growing crops.

He found here the perfect combination of soil and climate for the production of the choicest qualities of coffee ; of the most aromatic cacao ; of the sweetest sugar cane ; of the toughest rubber ; of the bluest indigo ; of corn, fruits, vegetables, and grasses. He found a vast park of the choicest woods—mahogany, ebony, cedar, rosewood, dye woods, and other varieties nearly as valuable ; a country within whose hills gold and silver abound.

In this natural garden he found a peon population as simple in their habits as were the occupants of the garden of biblical history ; a population whose food came without toil, and who never thought of clothing as a matter of comfort, who labored, if at all, on the homœopathic principle, and who contributed but little to the commerce of the world. He argued that, as these Indians, docile, listless, without aim or ambition, languished and died under a system of enforced labor, and the negro multiplied and waxed fat under a similar system, the substitution of the black for the bronzed race, would be wise and just.

Walker found a country rent by factions, marshalled by ambitious leaders, under whose alternate domination the public service was arbitrarily administered; a country whose population had been decreasing by reason of these factional wars, and whose once productive farms were on the road to ruin. Political parties, divided upon important questions of governmental policy, did not exist. Two political factions, one with headquarters at Granada, the other at Leon, pretended to govern the country, each under a different constitution. There was no government in the better sense of the word at that time; the people were divided into clans, which had no further significance than attachment to the ambitions of a chieftain; there was no peace, no tranquility, no security of person or property; a man was liable to be shot at any moment for being a traitor to one faction or another; the collection of revenue was nothing more than a process of garroting and bleeding. And, to be faithful to the truth of history, Walker's methods of government did not rise much above those theretofore prevailing. In carrying out his plan for supplanting the Spaniard with the Anglo-Saxon, he did not hesitate to confiscate and sell to his friends the estates of his political enemies. Even a distinguished United States Senator, who came to Nicaragua to advise with him, seemed to find it not inconsistent with his estimate of his high position to bid in a valuable cocoa hacienda at a figure much below its true value.

The expulsion of Walker was the turning point in the history of Nicaragua. From that time until 1893, the country had a stable government, and, in the main, an honest one. The people remained at peace with themselves and with their neighbors. During these years much land was brought under cultivation; many large coffee farms were opened and planted; modern machinery brought in for preparing the berry for market; sugar plantations successfully established, and public roads constructed. A railroad which, in connection with steamers on the lakes and the San Juan river, provides a public transit across the continent, was built and equipped by the government under President Càrdenas. A free-school system founded upon the general plan of free schools in the United States, has been established. Religious liberty has been secured under the administration of President Zelaya. A mail service is now managed by the government, and all parts of the Republic are fairly served. Telegraphs and telephones connect the principal towns, both managed by the government, and quite reasonable rates are secured.

Managua, the capital, has grown from an Indian village to a city of good buildings and considerable commerce; the production of coffee has increased from nothing to the value of nearly $2,000,000; the exports of bananas have kept a good race with those

A COFFEE YARD IN MANAGUA.

of coffee. Nicaragua cocoa has acquired a worldwide reputation for its high quality and delicious flavor. The Menier Brothers, of Paris, it will be remembered by visitors to the Columbian Exposition at Chicago, made a great advertisement of their 10,000 acres model cocoa plantation in this country. The Nicaragua devotee of chocolate will not hesitate to pay one dollar a pound for the home product in preference to accepting the cocoa sometimes imported from South America and offered at one-half that price. You can depend upon his judgment, or rather, that of his wife, as to the quality of cocoa. In the quality of its coffee, Nicaragua is equally fortunate. An Englishman, proprietor of a 1,500 hacienda, claimed, in a recent conversation with me, that as good coffee is grown in that country as either the Java or Mocha of commerce. Not being an expert in coffee, I do not vouch for this statement, but many other persons do claim for the Nicaraguan product a very high grade. Be this as it may, the average coffee planter in Nicaragua and Costa Rica considers himself in poor luck if he fails to realize out of his crop twenty-five per cent. to thirty per cent. net, on the money invested in his farm and machinery each year. The Englishman further remarked: "The elevation where I am located is exactly right for the production of a big crop of coffee; the soil of loam and volcanic matter is deep, apparently inexhaustible in fertility, and is composed of precisely the right elements compounded in correct proportions;

the rains come at the right time and in the proper quantities; the days are just hot enough, the nights just cool enough to maks perfect berries; the sun and the clouds perform their proper functions to perfection; the winds keep the air pure and healthy. I cannot see," he added, "wherein I could suggest an improvement upon the job of the Creator, in soil, climate or other natural conditions." This gentleman lives among the Sierras south of Managua—in the region which has given to this city its chief wealth. Her principal citizens own coffee farms in the same general section. And just beyond, where the alluvial plains are not much above the level of the lakes, are located the many plantations of cocoa, extending over to Rivas and beyond to the line of the Maritime canal.

Around Matagalpa, in the northern part of the Republic, is being developed an extensive coffee region. There any altitude desired can be had. The soil is as rich as the valley of the Red river of the North; the land is watered by many mountain streams; labor is abundant at fair wages. The climate is delightful. It is equable, seldom reaching 80 per cent. of heat. The trade winds in their sweep from ocean to ocean, are a security of healthfulness.

The chief banana development for commercial purposes is in what is known as the Musquito Territory. The Escondido river is navigable for ocean steamers some sixty miles above Bluefields. On both sides of this river and on up its branches for many miles further, bananas in sufficient quantities to load many ships each month of the year are grown, which are marketed in the States.

There are yet in Nicaragua thousands of square miles of lands suited to the culture of bananas, coffee, cocoa, sugar, rubber and rice, still covered with deep, dark, almost impenetrable forests. As in Walker's day there are thousands of natives still living in groups of huts, thatched with palms, surrounded by patches of corn, beans and plantains, who, philosophers in their way, think it better to enjoy life than to die rich. They prefer cock-fighting to labors of the field; and, so long as their daily wants are supplied, the morrow may care for itself. Generous, indolent, good-natured and improvident, they are true children of this sensuous clime, where open-handed nature would shame a grasping race. Missionaries would persuade them that man was made to labor and to mourn, but they prefer to loaf and to laugh. There is a flavor of Orientalism, a southern luxuriousness, a more than ordinary love of the bright and beautiful, among the race. Perhaps, in the lower classes, it touches the line of barbaric taste; but it, nevertheless, exists, and as refinement and education elevate, it develops into artistic qualities. No home is so humble as to be without flowers; few women so poor as to be without a bright-colored "rebozo" about their shoulders, even though they have little additional apparel. Notwithstanding their lack of fondness for work, the men are many grades superior to the universal tramp with whom civilization is now contending. Each succeeding year a greater number of natives join the ranks of labor in the coffee and banana fields. And year by year a greater number of the young men of the country go abroad to school or to travel, and come back with more liberal and progressive ideas, with new ambitions, and with these a greater fondness for American push and American progress. No longer do the intelligent people believe that the government of the United States was behind Walker in his raid or that the people of the Republic of the North desire either to conquer or annex them.

When we reflect upon the condition in which the people of Spanish America were at the close of their struggle for independence; in what dense ignorance they had been kept by their bestial oppressors; with what degrading superstitions the latter had filled their minds; with what barbarity they had been driven, robbed and murdered, we may well be astonished at the progress they have made rather than be disappointed that they have not done better.

The Nicaraguans look forward to the building of the Maritime canal to bring capital and enterprise to develop their lands. They have looked for the coming of this savior for, lo! these many years. Squier tells of an old lady who, as long as 1848, in trying to sell him a hut and ground on the banks of picturesque Managua lake for the modest sum of $100, offering to throw in her two plump daughters, added: "Los Norte Americanos are building a canal, and in a few months the property will be worth four times that money!" Another writer says: "Its inhabitants, high and low, have been praying in all tunes of their musical language to all the saints in the calendar, 'Ojalá que venga el canal,' and with it redemption from existing conditions. And when the long expected Messiah came they bound him hands and feet and cried 'crucify Him.'" But I believe the Nicaraguans will give the canal a genuine welcome.

Desiring to gather from intelligent native citizens of Nicaragua and Costa Rica and from the surviving contemporaries of Gen. William Walker some impressions of his personal appearance, habits, and career in Central America, as remembered by them, and to ascertain what measure of courage and ability they now accord him, after a lapse of forty years, I questioned several in person and wrote to others.

The first answer I received by mail was from an American who came to Nicaragua with Walker, and is a highly respected and successful business man there at this time. "A comrade and friend of Gen. Walker, it would be an agreeable task for me to tell you about this remarkable man. In my youthful enthusiasm I thought our chief was a hero, and though in after years I learned to judge his character more dispassionately I have no reason to change my general estimate of him. He was probably the greatest of all the soldiers of fortune."

From others I gather that, in personal appearance,

Walker was tall and handsome, with a muscular though slender frame and a commanding figure. His forehead was prominent, his lips firm, his big grey eyes keen and penetrating, and his well-set jaws indicated decision of character. His mind was active, alert, and exceedingly vigorous. In manner he was dignified and calm, suave, and winning; in action self-possessed and deliberate; in speech easy, fluent, and forceful. While he made no pretense to oratory, he had a faculty of stirring the souls of his followers and swaying the multitude when he addressed them. While kind to all and merciful to prisoners, he was strict in discipline, scrupulous in the observance of law, and stern in the enforcement of military decrees. His courage was unquestioned. He flinched from no duty; he evaded no responsibility. He was an ambitious, restless, daring man, but not a successful one. By turns he had been doctor, lawyer, journalist, politician, a military leader in an expedition into Mexico, prior to his campaign in Nicaragua, and he was yet a young man. He was a man of genius. His imagination was a gem of the first water. But I am impressed with the belief that not a majority of those whose opportunities of judging were best would award to Walker the possession of the higher qualities of a statesman or a military chieftain. At least, he did not exhibit the breadth of knowledge, the prudence, the sagacity, the calm, clear vision and force—that combination of qualities which go to equip a man for every emergency. But who can say that success were possible under any leadership?

Table of Contents.

	PAGES
INTRODUCTORY	3–18

GENERAL WILLIAM WALKER, OR THE WAR OF THE FILIBUSTERS.

Chapter I.

Picturesque Nicaragua.................................... 27–38

Chapter II.

Descent of Walker upon Nicaragua—"La Falange Americana"—Repulse at Rivas, June 29, 1855—Defeats Gardiola September 3, 1855................................ 39–48

Chapter III.

Granada captured by a *coup d'audace*, October 13, 1855—Treaty of October 23rd—Provisional Government—Don Patricio Rivas, President; Walker, Commander-in-Chief, 49–58

Chapter IV.

Costa Rica declares war—A new election decreed—Walker becomes Dictator—Rivas and Jerez abandon Leon and proceed to Chinandega—Central American alliance against Walker—First battle of Masaya, October 13, 1856—Second battle of Masaya, November 15, 1856 59–82

Chapter V.

Abandonment of the Occident—Defence of the Guadalupe—"Aqui fue Granada"—Spencer on his raft—The Transit closed—The Allies close around Walker at Rivas—He surrenders to Captain Davis of the United States war-schooner, *Saint Mary*, May 1, 1857 83-104

Chapter VI.

Walker makes another attempt against Nicaragua—Is arrested and brought back by Commodore Paulding, of the United States Navy—Is tried for a violation of American Neutrality laws and acquitted—His descent with ninety followers upon Truxillo, August 6, 1860, in Honduras—His surrender to Captain Salmon, of the British ship *Icarus*—Is delivered over to the Hondurans and condemned to death by General Don Mariano Alvarez—His death on the fatal "Cauquette"—Buried in the Campo Santo of Truxillo 105-118

THE NICARAGUAN CANAL.

Introductory note 121
Nicaraguan Canal 123-194

The Monroe Doctrine.. 197-216

ILLUSTRATIONS.

		PAGES
1.	WILLIAM WALKER .................................FRONTISPIECE.	
2.	MAP OF NICARAGUA	2–3
3.	A COFFEE-YARD IN MANAGUA	12–13
4.	THE PRINCIPAL STREET IN GREYTOWN................	30–31
5.	A WATER-CART IN RIVAS............................	42–43
6.	PEON'S CABIN, BREAD-FRUIT AND COCOANUT PALM....	54–55
7.	SCENE ON SAN JUAN RIVER	66–67
8.	RUINS OF AN ANCIENT CHURCH, GRANADA............	78–79
9.	MARKET PLACE, GRANADA	90–91
10.	GARDEN SCENE IN GRANADA.........................	102–103
11.	CEMETERY IN GRANADA	114–115
12.	CASTILLO, SAN JUAN RIVER	130–131
13.	THE BREAKWATER AT GREYTOWN—LOOKING SEAWARD.	144–145
14.	RAILROAD THROUGH THE SWAMP BACK OF GREYTOWN..	158–159
15.	DREDGES WORKING IN CANAL—LOOKING WESTWARD ..	172–173
16.	RAILROAD BRIDGE ACROSS BENARD CREEK............	186–186

War of the Filibusters.

General William Walker,
or
The War of the Filibusters

CHAPTER I.

PICTURESQUE NICARAGUA.

The student of American history finds in the conquest of Nicaragua, by William Walker, the filibuster, a startling episode in the progress of a country upon which the eyes of civilized America are now turned as upon the most interesting spot on the continent—perhaps in the world.

The peculiar circumstance which attracts this interest was doubtless that which then directed Walker's selection in the choice of a republic in which to inaugurate his scheme for the "regeneration of Latin America."

This all important circumstance is the fact that here is, so to speak, the waist of the continent, capable of being spanned by the commerce of the world.

At the time of Walker's venture, Cornelius Vanderbilt, sometimes called Commodore Vanderbilt, had conceived and executed a transit across the territory of Nicaragua for travel and transportation. What was known as the "Overland Route," from

Washington, say, to California, was a primitive conception, almost like Hannibal's crossing the Alps. Jefferson Davis might, without impropriety, be called the father of the Pacific railroads. In the Senate of the United States, he was the pioneer; and as Secretary of War, he ordered a survey to determine the best route for constructing such a railway, which he regarded as a military necessity.

When Walker conceived his dream of redeeming Nicaragua, there was prevalent in the United States a doctrine, the outgrowth of over-prosperity, called "Manifest Destiny." To thoughtful persons, given to tracing the genesis and progress of ideas, nothing could excite more decided interest than this sudden frenzy in the people of the United States to annex the remainder of the continent—especially when we consider that they were just on the verge of a life-and-death struggle to hold on to what they had

The doctrine of Manifest Destiny is supposed to have an accredited father in one of the greatest of our party leaders—Stephen A. Douglas.

I prefer to have it stated in the language of a statesman now living, and whose voice is still potential in the conduct of public affairs Succinctly, here is the doctrine:

"Examine your maps, commence at the mouth of the Rio Grande, trace along down through the waters of the bay of Vera Cruz, around that high headland of Yucatan, down through the Caribbean Sea, across the Tropic of Cancer into the Gulf of Darien; cross the Isthmus there into the Gulf of Panama, follow up the Pacific coast through twenty-two degrees of latitude to the boundary line of the treaty of 1854, and all within those limits is fastened to the interests and wrapped up in the destiny of American institutions by the great God whose hand shapes the continents of the earth, and scoops out its oceans, gulfs, and harbors. The great law of self-defence and national security, a law of nations paramount to all other laws, calls imperatively for the practical recognition of this fact in the diplomacy and legislation of the Government. The waters of the Gulf of Mexico on its northern and eastern coast now wash the borders of five States of the Union, and its tide rises to the wharf of the commercial metropolis of the South. Over on the opposite side lie the distracted States of Mexico, and lower down those of Central America. They would constitute an easy acquisition to any European power with sufficient boldness to defy the Monroe policy of this Government, and from that line of coast the hostile armaments of all Europe could be equipped in sight of American soil. If the American Union shall be preserved, its wisest statesmen will be the first to look steadily and boldly to these facts, and to shape the policy of the nation toward its lawful and inevitable expansion." *

Here, then, we have the cult of "Manifest Destiny," as portrayed by a western statesman of that era. The absorption of the Continent.

That Walker, when he started out, was a disciple of this school, seems manifest.

Fortunately, he was a literary man, sometime editor of a Democratic newspaper. A writer of rare lucidity and vigor. After escaping from Nicaragua, he published "The War in Nicaragua," and we have thus a singularly full and detailed account of his adventures, and the aims and ambitions which inspired them. Except for the accidental good fortune which placed this rare volume, now out of print, in my hands, I should never have undertaken

---

* Senator Voorhees.

the task before me, unless I had gone to Nicaragua and possessed myself of the information contained in the files of his organ—"El Nicaragua en se"—established by him in Nicaragua, and conducted under his auspices.

Walker has furnished us with the data which alone can justify a biography—namely, what did the hero himself say and do in the prosecution of his life-work? These actions and sayings constitute the mirror in which, as in a camera, is photographed the individual. Whatever is received at second hand, is open to suspicion.

I have suggested one consideration that determined the point which Walker selected as best for his invasion, namely the inter-oceanic highway which the Accessory Transit Company had established across the Isthmus from Greytown or San Juan del Norte, on the Atlantic or Caribbean Sea, to San Juan del Sur, on the Pacific, a distance something less than one hundred and seventy-five miles. Its route lay through the San Juan river and lake Nicaragua, along the southern border of the Republic, adjoining her neighbor, the Republic of Costa Rica. At an early day, after their independence, these Central American States, Honduras, Guatamala, San Salvador, Nicaragua and Costa Rica, had welded themselves together in a Federal Republic modeled after their more powerful neighbor of the north. The result of federation, however, was only discord and confusion, and secession and disintegration soon

THE PRINCIPAL STREET IN GREYTOWN.

followed, until in **1855** when Walker made his descent, not a vestige of the Confederation remained.

As late as **1839**, there seemed to be left in Central America some shadow of Federal authority. John L. Stevens, the celebrated traveller, it appears, was engaged in chasing this phantom upon some mysterious mission for the Government of the United States, the nature of which he fails to disclose.

The problems presented to humanity and civilization by Tropical America are replete with interest, and full of difficulty. The physical conditions of nature, have not these a mysterious and controlling influence over the character of the inhabitants? over the institutions of the country—over its progress and destiny?

Where volcanic peaks, now dormant, now active, answer to each other, through the heart of a tropical region, which is shaken also, by corresponding or consequential seismic vibrations; is not the heart of man there subject to like eruptive and violent demonstrations? Do, or do not, Rome and Syracuse from out their ruins visible from Vesuvius, and overlooked by Etna, speak a language akin to that of Leon and Granada, dominated as they are by the smoking heights of Mombacho and Masaya?

Humboldt, in describing these very regions, standing amid the overwhelming majesty of Nature and the Eternal Summer of organic life, points out the great advantages which the inhabitants of the

United States have over the Spanish Americans. He then proceeds to remark : " Internal dissensions are chiefly to be dreaded in regions where civilization is but slightly rooted, and where, from the influence of climate, forests may soon regain their empire over cleared lands if their culture be abandoned."

Let us devote our attention for a moment to Picturesque Nicaragua. Of the Central American Republics, she is the largest. According to Mr. Squier, her area, including the disputed Mosquito Coast, is about 60,000 square miles. The hand-book of American Republics (1891) places it, in round numbers, at 50,000, excluding such disputed territory. This is 14,000 miles less in extent than the two Virginias.

There are two distinct geographical divisions ; the Western, lying upon and encircled by the Pacific coast, and the Eastern, girdled by the Atlantic and its arm, the Caribbean Sea.

The Western division is essentially tropical, while the Northern and Eastern division displays many characteristics of the temperate zone.

It is the Western or Pacific coast that we shall have to traverse, in considering the invasion of General Walker. From the Bay of Fonseca and the magnificent harbor of Realejo, on the Pacific, southward to San Juan del Sur, and thence across a narrow strip of land to Rivas and Virgin Bay, on the Gulf of Nicaragua, the operations of Walker were confined.

Indeed, it may be said that on the Western or Pacific side only was the essential statehood of Nicaragua embraced.

At that date (1855), she had five distinct departments, the Meridional, Oriental, Occidental, the Septentrional of Matagalpa, and Septentrional of Sogovia;* these departments were subdivided into districts for municipal purposes. The districts were named from the principal towns therein respectively situated. Thus, we had Leon, Granada, and Rivas on the Pacific side, and Matagalpa and Segoria in the Northern department.

It was principally between these cities, Leon, Granada, and Rivas that Walker operated. Leon was farthest north, towards Honduras, and Rivas farthest south towards Costa Rica; while Granada was situated on the Lake between the two, being sixty-five miles south of Leon, and about thirty-five or forty north of Rivas. The population of Granada was put at 15,000, that of Leon at 35,000, and of Rivas at 4,000 inhabitants. The port of Realejo, on the Pacific, was about fifteen miles southwest of Leon, while that of San Juan del Sur was about half that distance from Rivas; the distance between the two harbors coastwise being about one hundred and twenty-five miles. Immediately north of this Peninsula, which stretched from the Bay of Fonseca to San Juan del Sur, lay the two magnificent inter-com-

---
*There was likewise the department of Guanacosta, lying south of the San Juan river, much of which was disputed territory between the adjacent republics—Costa Rica and Nicaragua.

municating lakes, Nicaragua and Managua, at an average of about one hundred and forty feet above the level of the Pacific Ocean. The waters of these lakes are drained by the river San Juan, commencing at San Carlos on Lake Nicaragua, and emptying into the Caribbean Sea at the Eastern port, called San Juan del Norte. This was the route of the Vanderbilt Transit Company, viz: from San Juan del Norte by the San Juan River to Fort San Carlos, on Lake Nicaragua, thence across the lake to Virgin's Bay, and thence across a narrow strip of land to San Juan del Sur—the total distance being something less than one hundred and seventy-five miles.

It was this Isthmus, engirdled by the Pacific on the west with one hundred and twenty-five miles of seacoast, and bounded on the east by the two great Lakes, that Walker selected as the scene of his operations in Central America. Sentinelled on the one side by a chain of volcanic peaks, many of them wreathed in smoke, and shaken on the other by the pulsations of the mighty Pacific, the intervening country is as full of natural beauty and as prolific in the productions of the soil, as any similar spot on the continent.

It is essentially an equinoctial region, and characterized by the marked features of tropical America. For summer, it has the wet season, from May to October, and for winter, the dry, extending from October to May. The atmosphere, observes Walker, is a fluid altogether different from the atmosphere of northern climates—as if a thin and vapory exhalation of opium, soothing and exhilarating by turns, was being mixed at intervals with the common elements of the air.

When, on his march from the Occidental Department to surprise and capture Rivas, at sunrise the American came in sight of Lake Nicaragua. Valle, a faithful Indian auxiliary and guide, exclaims simply: "Ometepec!"—without other phrase or emotion.

But Walker was awestruck and lost in admiration, as he beheld the tall and graceful cone of the grand volcano rising out of the bosom of the lake, like a giant taking his siesta, his sides covered with the dark verdure of the tropics—in repose, but liable to awaken at any moment.

Perhaps no equal extent of the earth's surface, remarks Mr. Squier, exhibits so many and such marked traces of volcanic action as that part of Nicaragua intervening between its lakes and the Pacific Ocean.

All of the travellers in this region describe the curious remains of former volcanic action. In some places near these craters the ground is encrusted with sulphur, and dried and baked by subterranean fires; in others, there are orifices from which steam rushes out violently, and with noise; in the nearer approach, pools or lakes of dark brown water are discovered, with monstrous bubbles, three or four feet high. In fine, it required no remarkable stretch of imagination on the part of the natives when they named the crater of Mt. Masaya "the Hell of Masaya," while they styled the smaller, and extinct, though still **smoking orifices**, "Infernillos" or Diminutive Hells.

The tropical vegetation so often described by travellers, presents the same general features in all the regions of equatorial America in such manner that when we follow Stephens (1839) and Ford (1891) in Nicaragua, we seem to be going up the same streams ascended by Agassiz (1868), in Brazil. A narrow opening with high perpendicular banks, covered with bushes, wild flowers and moss, roofed over with branches of large trees, sometimes interlacing from the opposite banks, and always covered with *lianes*—vines—more or less luxuriant in growth.

The peninsula we are considering produces all the staples of the tropics—coffee, sugar, cacao (chocolate-nut), bananas, and the rest. Columbus skirted along the eastern coast, and with a geographical instinct was persuaded that there was a connecting waterway to the Pacific.

Lord Nelson, then captain, occupied San Juan, and captured the castle by that name from the Spaniards in 1780.

Here are monuments and idols of the pre-Columbian era, and evidently of Aztec origin; and here, likewise, are the ruins of Mooresque Castillian structures, as melancholy as those of Babylon or Rome.

Here are ancient cities whose streets are paved

with the marble of their own decay, spacious **plazas**, lofty façades, with **turrets and** spires gorgeously ornamented with stuccoed figures, magnificent cathedrals, arched **and** covered bridges, stately palaces—all now ruins!

Ah! but the **laboring** peasant, the simple **husbandman**, paid for these **in their** day and generation just as the humble laborer and sturdy ploughman are paying for many an empty pageant of to-day.

Such, then, in brief and blurred outline was the Picturesque Physical **Nicaragua of 1855 ; a country** in which the **forces of nature agitate themselves in** an extraordinary manner, **superinduced, no doubt,** by their proximity to the sun.

In 1855, according to Squier, the population of Nicaragua was 300,000, distributed as follows: Whites, 30,000 ; **Negroes, 18,000 ; Indians, 96,000 ;** Meztizos, 156,000.

The Meztizos (which means in reality the Amalgamated races), it will be seen outnumbered all the individual **types combined.** The pure Indians were largely **preponderant in the northern** departments. Some of them constitute a hardy, unconquered race of people, **resisting and defying the domination of** the Spaniards, while **adopting their** religion. Nothing can **convey to our minds a** more realistic conception **of** Nicaragua **of 1855 than to suppose** that northern **New York,** for example, embracing half of the **State, were inhabited by a race** of unconquered Indians superior in **numbers to the** white population.

However, these unconquered savages, Indian *bravos,* as they were called, were beyond the region which we necessarily penetrate in the history of Walker. Walker's description of the native Indians in the latter region answers very accurately to that given by Agassiz of those he saw in Brazil. They are ignorant, simple, docile and easily imposed upon.* Walker was so impressed by these admirable qualities, that as we shall see, he proposed to utilize them by reducing these Indians to slavery.

" The people of Nicaragua (says Stephens) are said to be the worst in Central America, and they are proportionately devout."†

Another traveller tells us they are much darker in complexion than those of Costa Rica. Mr. Ford, however, dwells enthusiastically upon the *honesty* of the men and the homely virtues of the women as witnessed by him in San Juan. Not even the hackmen in that city are sufficiently civilized to cheat the tourist; a deficiency which certainly cannot be attributed to the cabmen of Washington or London.‡

Upon the whole, I think we may conclude that the native population with which Walker had to deal was about the same in character as that of other Latin-American republics—neither much better, nor manifestly worse.

---
* A journey to Brazil.
† 2 Stephen's Travels in Central America, &c., 19.
‡ Ford's Tropical Am., 380.

CHAPTER II.
1854.

DESCENT OF WALKER UPON NICARAGUA—LA FALANGE AMERICANA—REPULSE AT RIVAS, JUNE 29, 1855—DEFEATS GARDIOLA SEPTEMBER 3, 1855.

WALKER commences his narrative by an account of his descent with a small party of "Filibusters" upon Sonora in Mexico. He says that that invasion was instigated by a desire to protect the inhabitants of that state from hostile Indians; a proposition so preposterous and improbable, that did not the author's fatal earnestness of disposition forbid, we should think it intended for a grim bit of humor.*

His ventures against Mexico were closed by his surrender to an American military officer, after retreating before a greatly superior force of Mexicans, to whom he had given battle at La Paz.

The last remains of this unfortunate expedition reached San Francisco about the middle of May, 1854.

After almost insuperable difficulties, Walker and Cole succeeded in getting a liberal colonization grant, under which three hundred Americans were to be introduced into Nicaragua, "and were to be guaranteed forever the privilege of bearing arms."

This grant was from D. Francisco Castellon, Pro-

---
* The War in Nicaragua, 22.

visional Director of Nicaragua, and leader of the Democratic party. The republic was, as usual, in a state of revolution, the Democrats being represented as we have seen by Castellon, and the Legitimists by D. Jose Maria Estrada.

After a stormy voyage from San Francisco, in his vessel, the *Vesta*, Walker and his little band of fifty-eight adventurers, armed with rifles and revolvers, reached the port of Realejo on the 10th of June, 1855.

In the meantime the fortunes of Castellon had been much impaired since his grant to Cole and Walker in December, 1854.

Honduras, Costa Rica and Guatamala, having a temporary respite from domestic revolution at home, were paying some attention in a military way to the civil war in Nicaragua.

From the harbor Walker and his party were conveyed up the river five miles to the town of Realejo where they disembarked. In the ascent they passed over the very ground trodden by the great English buccaneer, Sir Henry Morgan. We may here pause to reflect that the same England that acquitted and knighted her own free-booter afterwards captured our American adventurer and turned him over to be shot.

Walker was received with open arms by Castellon, and the Americans were invited to enter his service as a separate corps, to be called " La Falange Americana"—The American Phalanx.

On the 20th of June, Walker received his commission as colonel in the Democratic army, and the Minister of War informed him that commissions would issue to others of his party as he might suggest.

This was accordingly done, and the Falange was organized into two companies. He remained inactive but three days, and at the expiration of that time he is found again on board the *Vesta*, with his Americans, and one hundred native troops, bound for Rivas in the Meridional Department, then in the possession of the Legitimists. The army of Estrada, the Legitimist, was commanded by General Corral, and that of Castellon, the Democrat, by General Muñoz. On the 27th of June, Walker landed at San Juan del Sur and made preparations to attack Rivas. On the 25th he captured the little village of Tapa, and on the 29th assaulted *Rivas*. The Legitimists, with about 500 men, were concentrated in the Plaza, and the Americans entered the town and took possession of the houses crowning the summit of the hill of Santa Ursula.

The native troops, under Colonel Ramirez, did not support Walker, but failed to advance. In the meantime the enemy was reinforced by seventy-five or eighty fresh troops from San Juan del Sur, under Colonel Arguello, and these falling on Walker's flank interposed themselves between him and the native Democrats, whereupon the latter incontinently marched away toward Costa Rica, leaving Walker to his fate. The gallant little band made a desperate sally, however, and made good their retreat. The fight lasted four hours, and of his handful of Americans Walker lost six killed, and twelve wounded, of whom five were left in the town, only to be captured and barbarously murdered. The enemy lost, some seventy killed and as many wounded. Walker had thus in less than a fortnight after his arrival sailed a distance of 125 miles, and lost more than one-fifth of his small band, including some of his bravest officers—Crocker and Kewen—killed, while Doubleday, Anderson, and De Brissot were wounded.

On the 30th of June the little band, numbering forty-five, reached San Juan del Sur in safety, though a good deal the worse for wear, but " still clinging to their rifles."

The *Vesta* not being in sight, Walker pressed into service a Costa Rican schooner, San José, and made his way back to sea, keeping a sharp look-out for his own brig, which he subsequently overtook.

While Walker was waiting to embark on the *San José*, two irresponsible persons, not connected with his command, set fire to the barrack of the Legitimists, just vacated by Colonel Arguello when he marched to the assistance of Rivas. One of these men was an American from California, and the other a drunken sailor called Sam. Walker having got possession of these men ordered them to be shot without any form of trial. Sam, however, escaped

from his guards, but Dewey, defying Walker's authority, was shot and killed.

Thus, before he had been in Nicaragua two weeks, our adventurer had given the natives two signal illustrations of traits which characterized his career—rashness and cruelty. It must be admitted, however, that when subsequently at San Juan del Sur, he ordered his surgeon to treat the wounded prisoners of war with the same care and attention bestowed upon his own wounded, contrary to the prevailing Central American custom of killing them on the spot, Walker taught the natives a much more salutary lesson.

When he got back to the port of Realejo, whence he had sailed, he made an elaborate report to Castellon of his proceedings, and openly accused General Muñoz, who had opposed the expedition, of bad faith, and charged that in deserting Walker at Rivas Ramirez had behaved treacherously at the instigation of Muñoz. Castellon was too hard pressed, however, to take up Walker's quarrels, and so he endeavored to patch up a truce between him and the commanding general. The opposing general, Corral, had advanced northward from Granada and was reported to have reached Managua at the head of 1,000 Legitimists.

Now, Managua is but fifteen miles from Granada and only forty from Leon, so that two days' forced march would bring him upon the Democratic capital. Walker was a very good ally to have on hand in such an emergency, as he was entirely unacquainted with fear and given to exaggerating, as with the wand of a wizard, his own resources. The people were likewise partial to the Americans, because they cherished the hope that their presence would ameliorate the horrors of the press-gang, that scourge of Tropical America.

The cholera had now broken out at Managua, and this proved a more efficient ally than Walker. If Corral had any real design of a speedy march upon the Democratic capital the ravages of the epidemic among his troops soon drove him back to Granada.

Walker had determined upon another expedition against the Meridional Department. His object was manifest; it was his fixed policy to get as near the *Transit* as possible, in order to recruit from the passengers to and from California, and to have the means of easy and rapid communication with the United States. As a preliminary step, he gave up his colonization grant and received in return authority to recruit 300 men who were to be paid one hundred dollars a month while in service, and a grant of five hundred acres of land at the close of the campaign.

About the middle of August, Walker got his Falange aboard the *Vesta* at the port of Realejo, together with his friend Vallé *alias* Chelon, at the head of from 160 to 170 native recruits, considerably weakened by desertion, however, and cholera. Vallé, who was a true Nicaraguan, did not like to let such a fine opportunity for counter-revolution escape **him**, and but for Walker's dissuasion would have erected his own Democratic standard, **and** the Red Ribbon of Chelon in opposition to that of Castellon.

On the 29th **of** August, the *Vesta* made the port of San Juan del Sur. She was too small to carry all of Walker's army, **and was** followed **by a** " ketch," (whatever that may **be), containing a portion of** the native volunteers.

Upon landing at **San Juan** del Sur, Walker **found** himself at the head of a force, consisting of fifty **Americans** and one hundred and **twenty** natives; a **number of the latter, however, sick with cholera, or** *colerin.*

From this period, say September 1st, commenced a series of brilliant achievements by our adventurer, which, had only *judgment* been vouchsafed him, must have assured a career of extraordinary brilliancy, if **not** of permanent success.

In some manner, not entirely explicable, one Gardiola, a professional revolutionist, distinguished by his cruel and bloodthirsty career, had descended from Honduras (for want of a convenient revolution at home, perhaps), to take **a hand in** the civil war of Nicaragua. **When Walker was in** the **Occidental Department, it** was rumored that Gardiola was in the north, and great apprehension prevailed at Chinandega, **where Walker was** encamped, of his descent upon that region. No sooner, however, does Walker **reach San Juan del** Sur than Gardiola appears at Rivas, and leaving there with six hundred chosen men; and learning of Walker's march to Virgin's Bay, the Legitimist captain follows close upon him, and finally coming up with him on the 3rd of September, vigorously attacks him in the town of Virgin, on Lake Nicaragua. Walker's disposition of his little force of 170 men seems to have been admirable. He had now the advantage of the barricades on his own side, and the deadly rifles of the Falange did fearful execution among the advancing Legitimists. Walker had his back to the Lake and his front to the foe, and nobody, not even the natives under Chelon *alias Vallé*, expecting any quarter at the hands of Gardiola, the struggle was to the death. Victory declared for the Democrats, and Gardiola retreated, leaving sixty dead on the field, while Walker had of the Falange only three or four wounded and none killed, and of the natives (who under the faithful Vallé behaved quite differently from their conduct at Rivas in June) two were killed and three wounded. Walker himself made a narrow escape, having been knocked down by a spent ball which struck him on the throat. It was here that Walker again exhibited a civilized example to the Nicaraguans, by directing every care and attention to be bestowed upon the wounded of the enemy who fell into his hands, notwithstanding the fact that Gardiola was supposed to fight under the black flag.

On the afternoon of September 4th, Walker conducted his troops back to San Juan del Sur, elated by victory, and enriched by over one hundred and fifty muskets, and considerable ammunition, taken from the enemy.

General Muñoz (who seems to have been a pretty considerable man, notwithstanding Walker's dislike to him), had defeated Gardiola at Savce in the Occidental Department, but had died of a wound received in the engagement.

And now Castellon, worn out by the cares and vexations of revolution, succumbed to the prevailing scourge, just as Walker's courier arrived with the glad tidings of his victory.

Castellon was a man of confiding, gentle nature, much beloved and respected by his followers.

He was succeeded in the Provisional Directorship by D. Nasario Escoto, being the senator designated for the office by the Constitution of 1838.

At this point, in the outset of his career, Walker set another worthy example to the Nicaraguans. He would receive of native troops only *volunteers*, and refused the *forced levies* which were, and still are, the curse of Latin-America. He discouraged also the seizure of private property by impressment.

The native troops, therefore, which the Provisional Director forwarded to San Juan del Sur were but few. On the other hand, many recruits—Democrats and exiles—began to join Walker's standard in the Meridional Department.

There was still another very bad practice prevalent in Nicaragua, which Walker found himself obliged to adopt, and that was forced contributions from business men and traders to carry on the campaign. While deprecating the necessity, he excuses himself by saying that "reforms in revenue," as to the method either of raising or collecting it, cannot well be attempted in the midst of war.

The wisdom of his policy in establishing himself in close proximity to the Transit now became apparent.

Recruits were obtained from the passengers to and from California, until by the middle of September he had in his Falange sixty effective men, while Vallé, in spite of loss by cholera, had over two hundred native troops. On the 3d of October, one Col. Charles Gilman, a companion of Walker in lower California, who had lost a leg there, arrived with thirty-five stalwart recruits from California.

In the meantime Corral had come from the Occidental Department, and assumed command of the Legitimists at Rivas.

CHAPTER III.
1855.

GRANADA CAPTURED BY A COUP D'AUDACE, OCTOBER 13, 1855—TREATY OF OCTOBER 23D—PROVISIONAL GOVERNMENT—DON PATRICIO RIVAS, PRESIDENT; WALKER, COMMANDER-IN-CHIEF.

WALKER now conceived the design of capturing Granada, the capitol of the Legitimists, not for permanent occupation, but to gain vantage ground whence he could treat for peace on better terms.

Accordingly, he marched to Virgin's Bay, and there awaited the arrival of *La Vergen*, a steamer of the Transit Company, engaged in transporting passengers and freight across the Isthmus. Nothwithstanding the protest of her captain, Walker embarked all of his force, and after employing every precaution to conceal his movement from Corral, who was still at Rivas, he landed his troops on the night of the twelfth of October, and early the next morning entered Granada. The Granadinos were taken completely by surprise, and although there were but few troops there, Walker was enabled to capture many distinguished adherents and officials of the party of the Legitimists. These, old Chelon, *alias* Vallé, proposed at once to shoot, in retaliation for a similar favor the Legitimists had done to one of the old Indian's brothers. But Walker sternly interdicted all executions, and put a very peremptory stop to everthing like pillage or disorder. It must have struck the inhabitants that after all the scheme of the lamented Castellon *"for the regeneration of Nicaragua by the introduction of a new element"* was beginning to realize the dream of a better civilization.

The United States minister, Hon. John W. Wheeler, resided in Granada, and he consented to act for Walker as one of a commission to wait upon Gen. Corral and negotiate for terms of peace. This commission reached Rivas about the middle of October, but found that Corral had marched North on the afternoon of the fourteenth. This interposition on Wheeler's part, Corral highly resented, and the former returned to Granada without an interview. The other commissioners met Corral on his march northward and communicated to Walker that it was impossible to get Corral to treat on any terms whatever.

In a few days Walker was reinforced by a party of sixty filibusters from California, commanded by Parker H. French and Col. Birkett D. Fry, the latter a veteran of the Mexican War. These people came from Virgin Bay to Granada in a vessel belonging to the Transit Company, doubtless, so used under compulsion, as had been "the Virgin" by Walker. This so incensed the Legitimists that their soldiers committed sundry outrages upon the American passengers at Rivas, plundered the building of the Transit Company, and from Fort San Carlos fired upon one of the steamers with fatal effect.

Walker in retaliation for these outrages ordered one of his most distinguished prisoners, Mayorga, a member of Estrada's cabinet, to be shot, which order was promptly executed on the Plaza at Granada on the twenty-second of October.

This murder of Mayorga led to consequences much more fortunate for all parties than could have been anticipated. For no sooner did the intelligence reach Corral, who had now entered Masaya, and was behind its barricades, than he and the other Legitimists, many of whom had friends and relatives in Granada, began to sue for peace. Accordingly, on the twenty-third of October Corral and Walker agreed upon the terms. On the part of the Legitimists Corral had full powers—*omnimodamente*—to execute the treaty, but on the part of the Democrats it had to be sent to Leon for ratification.

In due time, however, it was confirmed at the Democratic capitol, and became the law of the land. By its terms Walker was to be placed at the head of the army, and all the other officers on both sides were to retain their existing rank and pay. The Americans were to be retained in the service of the Republic, and the debts contracted by either party were to be provided for. At Walker's suggestion the articles of the Constitution of 1838, concerning naturalization, were to remain in force. This must have been inserted out of abundant caution, since there was no suggestion from any quarter that the Constitution should be abrogated, or in any manner impaired. The white and red ribbons were to be thrown aside, and the troops of the Republic were to wear a blue ribbon with the device—

NICARAGUA INDEPENDIENTE.

Don Patricio Rivas, a man of moderate political views, but inclined toward the Legitimists, was made Chief Executive under the new Provisional Government, to remain such for fourteen months, unless his successor was sooner elected. The treaty was ratified amid great popular acclaim, and with all due solemnities of religion, Walker and Corral knelt side by side and swore to observe and cause to be observed the treaty of October the 23d, 1855. Rivas assumed his new duties as Provisional President, and appointed Corral Minister of War, and also Premier, or Chief Minister. On October 31st, General Jerez arrived from Leon, accompanied by other prominent Democrats. The new Cabinet was completed, there being one American in it, Parker H. French, who was made minister of Hacienda, or, as we would say in the United States, Minister of Agriculture.

The other Cabinet officers were Jerez, Minister of Foreign Relations, and Ferrer, Walker's late Prefect, Minister of Public Credit.

The point now reached, being the acme of Walker's fortunes, is an appropriate one whence to take a retrospect of what he has accomplished. It is now but four months and a half since he landed at

Realejo in the Occident at the head of fifty-eight American adventurers, with nothing in his pocket but a land grant for colonization. In these four and a half months he has invaded the Meridional Department and fought two pitched battles, in the latter of which he signally defeated an experienced general of the Legitimist army, and captured large stores of small arms and ammunition. He next embarks his whole force on a steamer, which he runs past the enemy and almost under his guns, and by a forced march surprises and captures the capital city of the Granadinos without loss to himself, but with fatal damage to the Legitimists, in the important stores and prisoners secured, but above all in the prestige which he acquired by such bold, rapid and successful operations. He finds himself now at the head of nearly 600 volunteers—American and native—with no conscripts and no traitors in his ranks. He negotiates a peace whereby he is made Commander-in-chief of the Army of the Republic. In the new Provisional administration, his friends preponderate in the Cabinet, in the proportion of three to two. He has, moreover, relieved the Transit of the presence of all menace and obstruction, for even before the proclamation of peace the garrisons at San Carlos and Rivas have disappeared.

Now, or never, are those roseate visions of a regenerated Nicaragua, to be redeemed by the "infusion of the new element," and to lift themselves above the horizon of doubt and incredulity. If our hero has the stuff of which great men are moulded, from the pinnacle now attained, achievements worthy of civilization will avouch that immortality, which

"All-telling Fame doth noise abroad."

On the 5th of November, amid the general rejoicing at the return of peace, a startling event occurred well calculated to shake the stability of the *modus vivendi* which had taken shape in the new Provisional Government.

General Corral, late at the head of the Legitimist armies, had been chiefly instrumental in drawing up the treaty of October 23d. Both he and Walker had sworn to obey its terms. One of its conditions was that Martinez, the Legitimist general, should remain in command at Managua, and Zatruch at Rivas. On November the 5th, Vallé brought to Walker intercepted communications sent by Corral, the new Minister of War, to General Gardiola, who, along with General Zatruch, had fled to Honduras.

There can be no manner of doubt that these letters were directly aimed at the destruction or expulsion of the Americans; that their spirit was in violation of the new treaty, and hostile to the new government; and as they called for assistance from other Central American States, it may not be doubted that they were overt acts of treason. Walker, as commander-in-chief of the army, summoned a court-martial, by whom Corral was arraigned, convicted and sentenced to be shot. The court, which by the choice of the defendant himself, was composed en-

PEGS'S CABIN, BREAD-FRUIT TREE AND COCOANUT PALM.

tirely of Americans, unanimously recommended the minister to mercy. The principal citizens, including many ladies of distinction, waited upon Walker and united in the recommendation of the court. The daughters of the accused fell upon their knees before him and besought his mercy. But he remained inexorable, and at two o'clock in the afternoon of November the 9th, the rifles are heard to ring out on the Plaza, and the "New Element" has proved itself a convert to the practices of the "Old Regime."

The vacancy occasioned by the death of Corral was filled by the appointment of D. Buenaventura Salva, a Democrat, so that the new ministry, with one exception, was composed entirely of Walker's friends.

On the 10th of November, the new provisional government was recognized by Mr. Wheeler, the Minister of the United States.

But now, just at the very threshold of the new administration, a blunder in policy is conceived and executed, under Walker's auspices, which in due season let loose the winds of Æolus, whose howl became the Iliad of all his woes.

To maintain himself in Nicaragua, it was absolutely essential that Walker should receive accessions of Americans, and these could only be introduced by way of the Transit across the Isthmus from San Juan del Norte to San Juan del Sur. This route had been opened in connection with a concession to a company of Americans made for the purpose of connecting the two oceans by a ship canal.

There were two companies, one owning the concession, or franchise (as we would say), called the Atlantic and Pacific Ship Canal Company, and the other the Accessory Transit Company, the latter holding the relation to the main corporation of the modern "Construction Company." The construction of this canal was an enterprise which every loyal citizen of the United States should encourage, and which no true American would oppose. Had Walker had the sublime ideal of a redeemed and regenerated Nicaragua really and sincerely at heart he would have realized the importance of the construction and opening of this great artery through which the pulsations of two oceans would give renewed vitality to the commerce of the world. This enterprise presented an opportunity of advancement far greater than any which he or Castellon or Rivas had devised, or were capable of executing.

So far, however, from rising to the height of the grand argument, Walker regarded the Inter-Oceanic canal in the light only of an adjunct to his own filibustering scheme of self-aggrandizement and power.

At the instigation of one or two personal friends in San Francisco representing the interest of a projected new company, he entered into a conspiracy to declare the charter of the canal company forfeited, and to seize their property and place it in the hands of a commission of his own selection. His course in this matter was utterly unjustifiable either under the Constitution of 1838 or under the laws which regulate international comity in civilized communities.

Except in countries absolutely despotic, there is no authority to annul charters by executive decree, and, still less, to seize private property or appoint commissions to hold, administer, convert or distribute it. All this is matter of judicial cognizance, and the exercise of any such authority by the executive is usurpation, and in the highest degree tyrannical and oppressive. The Constitution of November 12th, 1838, divides the government into three departments, and defines the duties of each; and Walker, who had been a student of law, must have known that in giving to executive "decree" the authority of a judicial inquisition, or legislative enactment, he was trampling the constitution of his adopted country under his feet. In due time it will appear what bitter fruit this high handed measure bore for its unfortunate projector. When these unjustifiable proceedings had been concluded, Walker proposed his new charter, and submitted it to President Rivas.

That there was a commercial deal in these transactions, conducted upon a low personal plane, must have become apparent to Rivas, prematurely for the designs of Walker, for we are told that the Provisional President signed the new charter, which dated February 19, 1856, with extreme reluctance.

To show the folly of Walker's conduct toward the Accessory Transit Company, we may mention that

Cornelius Vanderbilt, its president, just before the destruction and confiscation of his property, shipped at his own expense two hundred and fifty recruits to reinforce Walker's army. This was the friend, a prince of financiers, whom our short-sighted adventurer exchanged for some obscure friends of his own, who finally deserted and abandoned him, even before their own lamentable failure had lost to Nicaragua and to the world all present prospect of the execution of the most important work of modern times. Had Vanderbilt been let alone, it is probable that his genius might have accomplished this great work, now again (1895) in process of construction.

Notwithstanding this stupendous blunder, Walker's fortunes continued to thrive until in March, 1856, he numbered 1,200 Americans—citizens and soldiers under his command or influence—in Nicaragua. With a cool, deliberate pilot at the helm, the vision of regeneration, or at least palpable reform, ought now to have shaped itself clearly above the horizon as something capable of substantial realization—"a dream that was not all a dream."

Among the first acts of the new commander-in-chief was to disband the native Nicaraguan troops, and thus leave the military arm of the republic in the control of the Americans. Now, as the latter were all Democrats, this action would seem to be in violation of, if not the letter, at least the spirit of the new treaty.

It needs no further comment to show the extreme imprudence and impolicy of such a proceeding.

CHAPTER IV.
1856.

COSTA RICA DECLARES WAR—A NEW ELECTION DECREED—WALKER BECOMES DICTATOR—RIVAS AND JEREZ ABANDON LEON, AND PROCEED TO CHINANDEGA—CENTRAL AMERICAN ALLIANCE AGAINST WALKER—FIRST BATTLE OF MASAYA, OCTOBER 11TH, 1856—RELIEF OF GRANADA, OCTOBER 13TH, 1856—SECOND BATTLE OF MASAYA, NOVEMBER 15TH, 1856.

The Republic under her new auspices had sent, through General Jerez, Minister of Relations, the terms of the treaty of October 23rd, with friendly greetings, to the several Central American Republics. To this circular only one State, San Salvador, returned a favorable response. The others maintained an ominous silence. Many Legitimists of Nicaragua had taken refuge in Costa Rica, including Generals Zatruch and Martinez.

Through the agitation of these and other influences a very hostile feeling towards the new order of things in her northern neighbor was soon developed in the little republic.

She soon began active preparations for war, and was furnished arms and encouraged in her hostile demonstrations by the government of England. Similar hostile elements existed in the other republics. Honduras had just driven into exile her Liberal president, General Trinidad Cabañas, and no less person than General Gardiola was canvassing there to succeed in the presidential office. The professional revolutionist of Central America is like the professional politician in the United States, when defeated in one quarter he turns up somewhere else, with the irrepressible audacity of a loon of the Adirondacks, or an *ignis fatuus* of the Dismal Swamp.

On the 1st of March, 1856, Costa Rica formally declared war against the "Filibusters" in Nicaragua.

The president and leading spirit of Costa Rica was D. Rafael Mora, a man of supreme energy, and by nature as well as habit a revolutionist.

His declaration of war was not against the State of Nicaragua, but distinctly against the colonized Americans, whom he designated as "Filibusters." In this declaration he raised and flourished the black flag, declaring that all prisoners taken with arms in their hands were to be shot. It may be appropriate here to remark that during the late war between the United States there arose ever and anon a hoarse cry upon either side for the black flag! This was resisted by military men*, and was regarded by moderate men of all parties as the echo of semi-civilization.

Let us see how General Walker was prepared to meet the threatened invasion, which was aimed directly against himself and his American "Filibusters."

---

*Among the original black flag idiots was General Fremont, whom Mr. Lincoln rebuked. See Van Buren's Lincoln, page 116.

On the 1st of March, 1856, the regular American force in the service amounted to six hundred men. In addition to these there were several irregular bodies of men along the line of the Transit Company, amounting to about six hundred more, whom Walker thought could be relied upon for defensive purposes in case of foreign invasion.

About the 9th of March two hundred and fifty fresh recruits arrived under direction of one Goicouria, who was a Cuban, and in some way connected with the Transit, and interested in Walker in a manner commercial rather than military. On the 11th of October, Walker organized the new recruits into a battalion of five companies and placed them under command of Colonel Schlessinger.

On the same day (March 11th, 1856,) the General-in-Chief issued a proclamation declaring war against the Legitimist party, and called upon the army to throw aside the Blue Ribbon of October 23rd and resume the Red Ribbon of Democracy.

General Walker, ever ready to act on the offensive, determined to strike the first blow. There is in the department of Guanacaste, which lies in the South, immediately binding upon Costa Rica, much territory disputed between the two adjoining republics. It was towards this territory that Walker sent a force which was to intervene between the army of General Mora and the Transit, it being a matter of deadly importance to Walker to protect the Inter-oceanic communication, whence his recruits were to be introduced. With this view, General Walker sent his newly arrived battalion, under the command of Colonel Schlessinger, consisting of two hundred and forty men, divided into four companies, into the Meridional Department. Two of these companies were American, and of the remaining two one was German and the other French, with captains corresponding to these respective nationalities. It was on the 16th of March Schlessinger reached San Juan del Sur.

On the 20th he had reached what Walker styles the "country-house"* of Santa Rosa, which is in Costa Rica about a day's march south of San Juan del Sur. Here Schlessinger was surprised, defeated, and his battalion dispersed by the advanced forces of Mora's army of Costa Ricans.

All of the Nicaraguans who were captured were put to death without remorse—nothing being permitted to intervene between them and their fate except that murderer's phrase "Court-martial" or "Military Commission."

So ended the first expedition of the war with Costa Rica. The incompetent Schlessinger was put upon trial, but managed to desert and escape punishment.

This unfortunate disaster to his army at their outset had a most discouraging effect upon Walker's followers. Desertions and applications for furloughs were beginning to deplete his ranks. He determined to carry his army southward towards the seat of war, and to establish his headquarters at Rivas, in the

---
*On the maps it is put down as a town.

Meridion. This he accordingly did before the 1st of April, and the seat of government was at the same time removed from Granada to Leon. Before leaving Granada, however, the Provisional President issued a decree placing the Meridional and Oriental Departments under martial law, whereby, as to these departments, Walker was made substantially Dictator.

On March the 30th Walker had his whole army concentrated at Rivas, and there addressed them on the Plaza in language which seemed to inspire new confidence and put a check to despondency and desertion.

Meanwhile, his capital blunder in destroying Vanderbilt's transit began to bear its legitimate fruit.

Not a recruit has reached him since Cornelius Vanderbilt sent, at his own expense, the battalion of two hundred and fifty men.

The transit had become apparently useless to General Walker, and as the Occidental Department was being threatened from the north by Guatamala, he determined to march or sail back to Leon. Accordingly, on the 5th of April he embarked all his force on the steamer *San Carlos*, and on the 8th all were disembarked safely at Granada. No sooner had Walker left Virgin Bay than General Mora, who had crossed the frontier without Walker's knowledge, moved forward and took possession of the town. Here his troops fired upon the American laborers employed by the Transit Company, and broke open and robbed the Company's building and burned their wharf to the water's edge. Walker at Granada, hearing of these proceedings by Mora, determined at once to reverse his steps and attack Mora in Rivas. The very next morning after landing, on the 9th of April, Walker, at the head of 550 Americans, marched out of Granada at daylight and took the road to Rivas. Walker had discharged and disbanded all soldiers that could not speak English—a proceeding which would seem to be unwise in the extreme. He had left at Rivas a small body of native troops, and these, under command of one Machado, a Cuban, escaped Mora and rejoined Walker on his march. On the morning of April 11th Walker assailed Rivas, taking the Costa Ricans entirely by surprise. The number of the latter under Mora was estimated at three thousand—no doubt an overestimate.

Walker's information enabled him to locate the headquarters of the Costa Rican general, and his plan of attack was to concentrate around the house occupied by Mora, and, if possible, capture him in person.

The attack was led by Lieutenant-Colonel Sanders on the north of the Plaza with four companies, and Major Brewster with three companies on the south, while Colonel Natzmer with the Second Rifles was to threaten the enemy's right flank while he kept in supporting distance of Sanders.

Machado, with the natives, was to enter the Plaza on the north and to the right of Sanders, while Colonel Fry's light infantry was to be held in reserve.

The attack was well planned and gallantly executed. In a short time the Americans had full possession of the Plaza and all the houses around it. The Costa Ricans took refuge in the western portion of the town and fortified themselves in the adobe houses, through which they cut loop-holes for defensive firing.

The American troops with their rifles did deadly execution, but they could not be brought to storm the houses in which the enemy had taken refuge. The latter did not remain entirely on the defensive, but made one or two unsuccessful sallies after the Americans had ceased to advance.

When night came on both parties seemed to be exhausted, and Walker having no artillery and despairing of storming the barricades of the Costa Ricans determined to withdraw his force. With due precaution and silent deliberation, shortly after midnight, the command left the Plaza and the town, the wounded in the centre, and Major Brewster commanding the rear guard.

The Costa Ricans never discovered the departure till after daylight, when they had crossed the river Gil Gonzales, near Obraje. That night the command encamped again on the banks of Ochamago Walker's loss in the action was fifty-eight killed and sixty-two wounded, in all, counting those missing, about 120 men. He estimates that of the enemy at about 200 killed and 400 wounded. On the Serapagui the Costa Ricans, about 250 strong, were cutting a road to the San Juan river, to cut off Walker's communications, when they were, on the 10th of April, attacked and routed by an inferior force under Captain Baldwin. They retreated back to San José.

After his return to Granada, Walker had Father Vigil, a worthy Catholic priest, appointed as Minister to the United States by the Rivas administration. The good father repaired to Washington, and on reaching there was recognized by the American Government.

The attack on Rivas, while unsuccessful in redeeming the Meridional Department from the Legitimists and Costa Ricans, was, as an exhibition of bold and dashing military operations, of great service to the Americans. They had marched forty miles and surprised the enemy in his barricades, inflicting severe punishment; had returned in good order, and with but slight loss compared with that of the enemy.

The march of Mora northward was effectually checked, and his adherents much demoralized.

About the 21st of April, 200 new recruits were brought in by General Hornsby, and twenty volunteers were added, who had come to join Walker at their own expense.

Although the General-in-Chief had obeyed the instincts of humanity in his treatment of defenceless sick and wounded prisoners, yet his arbitrary character could not let the occasion of his regaining the Meridional Department go by without some irregular

SCENE ON THE SAN JUAN RIVER.

and unlawful execution. Accordingly, Francisco Ugarte, a leader of the Legitimists, was seized, tried by a "military commission," and sentenced to be hung—a mode of execution *"unusual in the country,"* says Walker, *"shooting being resorted to rather than hanging."*

We have now reached another crisis in the history of Walker in Central America.

In October, 1855, he had beaten the army of the Legitimists before Rivas, and compelled them to sue for peace. Now, has the tide of his adverse fortune turned in his favor by dashing itself against the ancient capital of the Meridion. The attack of the 11th of April, though apparently a defeat, bore the fruit, not of a single victory, but of a successful campaign. Not only were the Costa Ricans expelled and humiliated, but in the north and east in Segovia and Chantales—the plots of the Legitimists are quelled, and Mariona Salazar, who has been sent as commissioner to Matagalpa and faithful old Vallé, who has been rewarded by a similar appointment, both report entire order and submission to the Rivas administration in the northeastern or temperate latitudes of the Republic. Father Vigil, a Democrat, has been appointed Minister to the United States, and what is more to the purpose, has been recognized by the Great Republic of the North.

Walker, as General-in-Chief of the army, seemed now to enjoy the confidence of the natives, and is still receiving recruits from America. His maintenance of order in Nicaragua, and with it, a new departure in Central American civilization, depend now entirely upon himself.

Fortunately for history, he has furnished us in the clearest and most accurate English, the form into which his policy and designs at this crisis had developed themselves.

(1.) Although, as I have intimated, Walker was originally, perhaps, a disciple of the Manifest Destiny cult, yet now that he has met with success, he distinctly, almost scornfully, repudiates all idea of annexation.

(2.) As for Republicanism and Civil Liberty, he has not retained a vestige of veneration or regard for them. His maxim of government for Nicaragua is that "there can be but one head." His ideal is the "Military Republic," in other words, that child of Anarchy, called Dictatorship, is to this genuine convert to Central American methods, the only government for Nicaragua.

(3.) We are not left long in doubt as to the nomination and selection of this Dictator. Walker himself is to be the Santa Anna of Nicaragua.

(4.) Slavery is to be introduced. Perhaps of all the rampant vagaries of American political agitators of the nineteenth century, two forms will stand out most prominently, like the Pillars of Hercules, between which the seas of disorder and the waves of faction have lashed themselves to fury. One of these is Abolitionism and the other that offspring of Abolitionism, called the Slave Propaganda. To the professional office-seeker in the United States, ideas, platforms, principles, are only the hobby-horses whereby men may ride into power. But under their persistent stump oratory a few persons, generally esteemed cranks, begin to think their indoctrination sincere, and hence they advance upon *action* as the fruit would follow the blossom.

So it was that John Brown not only became possible, but advanced from the criminal classes to the ranks of the saints.

And so our poor unfortunate adventurer, after having coined everything but his heart's blood into the most astonishing career on record, begins from fighter to turn philosopher.

(5) Not only does this achiever of astonishing triumphs seek to reintroduce slavery into Nicaragua, but he tells us that the native Indian would prove the full equal of the negro as a slave, in docility and behavior, and could no doubt be readily reduced to that relation. In order to further this idea—really incapable of language—Walker repeals all ordinances which precede the Constitution of 1838, including that which prohibited slavery.

Our adventurer, however, overlooked the fact that the Constitution of 1838 did itself prohibit slavery, in any form whatever.

But I am persuaded that my readers of the narrative of this Central American John Brown are now prepared to understand the causes of his failure. He was a man capable of producing great opportunities, but without the power to subdue them.

It was necessary to group these principles and designs of Walker in advance of his own narrative, in order to understand the unfolding of events in Nicaragua, and especially his abandonment by the Democratic party, at whose invitation he had entered the Republic, and whose crimson colors decorated his army.

Being a fearless, outspoken man, there can be no doubt that the prominent men of all parties began to understand something now of his real designs, and the methods by which he proposed to accomplish them. What he calls "the defection of Rivas" would appear a most natural and patriotic proceeding, when the lofty ambition and real character of Walker were revealed to the Provisional President.

About the period we have reached—say June 9th, 1856—rumors were authentic that President Carrera, of Guatamala, had sent a large force southward, then on the march against Nicaragua. This fact Rivas made the subject of proclamation to the people, published on June the 3d.

It may not be amiss at this point to inquire who this Carrera was, that his name should inspire such terror in Central America. There can be no doubt that since the historic era, from the aboriginal stock there has sprung no man at all comparable to Carrera.* In the north we have had Philip, Black Hawk and Tecumseh, and in the south we have golden myths of Montezuma and Guatemozin. But it was reserved for Carrera alone to take up successfully the gage of battle for his native race, to be hailed by them as their savior.† To bring to his feet the old Spanish aristocrats, to defend the church, to organize government, evoke order out of chaos, and subduing the restless elements of a mixed Central American population, to remain steadily at the helm of state for fourteen consecutive years. The regret that all must experience is that this truly great man has had no historian, and like so many others, is as yet only to be seen as depicted by his enemies. His career had commenced under a flag inscribed " Death to whites, foreigners and heretics."

Mr. Squier, who visited Central America about this time, places the peace footing of Carrera's army at 1,550 men, and 125 officers; but adds that in an emergency 10,000 men could be raised in the Republic. Such was the army, and such the captain that was threatening Nicaragua from the north.

Walker concentrated his command at Granada, and having now thoroughly mastered the science of government as administered in Central America, he issued a pronunciamento constructing a new provisional government, with his old friend, D. Ermin Ferrer at its head. Rivas rescinded his election

---
* Unless we should except President Diaz. of Mexico.
† Squier, 514, 517.

decree, which Walker had forced upon him; but in the Oriental and Meridional Departments, the election was proceeded with, and the commander-in-chief was chosen, and on the 12th of July, ceremoniously inaugurated as president of Nicaragua.

In his pronunciamento, Walker had based his action upon the treaty of October 23d, which he had sworn to obey and cause to be obeyed, but he conveniently overlooked the fact that the treaty expressly recognized the Constitution of 1838, (which the contracting parties had no power to abrogate, even if so inclined), which, modeled after that of the United States, required the *president to be a native of the Republic*. Neither do we hear anything more about those representatives and senators, who were to be elected at the same time.

A few of the leaders among the natives adhered to Walker's fortunes, notably the faithful old Indian, Vallé. But a large majority joined the allies along with Rivas, Jerez, and Salazar. The last named having subsequently fallen into Walker's hands was forthwith shot by his order in the Plaza of Granada, doubtless, near the very spot where Corral was executed in the same way a few months before. Upon this coincidence Walker remarks with grim satisfaction: "There was the same joyful feeling shown by the old Legitimists at the death of Salazar as had been shown by the Democrats at the execution of Corral."

In the latter part of June and 1st of July, Walker received over 200 new recruits from various sections of the United States. He also seized a Costa Rican schooner, the *San José*, and converted her into a vessel of war called the *Granada*. Armed with two six-pound carronades she was placed under command of Lieutenant Faysson, a native of Missouri, and an adventurer, but of high courage and ability.

The forces of the allies were under the command of General Ramon Belloso, a San Salvadorian, and numbered probably 1,800 men, namely 500 from Guatamala, 500 from San Salvador, and 800 native Nicaraguans. The Guatamalans, under General Paredes, were nearly all Indians.

Walker ought to have had from 700 to 800 Americans under him. As early as the month of August, however, he begins to complain that desertions were thinning his ranks, though these were principally confined to the Europeans whom he had enlisted.

The Republic was now blessed with only three presidents: Walker in the Meridional Department, with headquarters at Granada; Rivas in the Occidental, at Leon; and Estrada, the Legitimist, who, after having taken refuge in Honduras, had again stepped upon the revolutionary stage, and was *starring*, so to speak, in the Septentrional regions, with headquarters at a mountain village called Samoto Grande. The situation was somewhat relieved, however, by the early murder of Estrada by a band of Democrats from Leon, who came upon him in his mountain retreat unawares. Thereafter the Legitimists gave in their adherence to President Rivas.

If ever there was a time in which a ruler needed to conciliate his people and weld them together in the bonds of a common patriotism, Walker had reached that crisis in the course of his affairs.

So far, however, from yielding to these dictates of rational judgment, the new President, surrounded by a cabinet of shadows, the Premier being his old Prefect, Ferrer, enters forthwith upon his schemes by promulgating a series of most despotic and extraordinary decrees, every one of which was calculated to alienate his people, outrage their feelings, and concentrate all Central America against him.

The first of these decrees was intended practically to substitute the English language for the Spanish in all public and official proceedings.

Then came a decree declaring the property of all enemies of the State forfeited to the Republic, and a board of commissioners was appointed to take possession of and sell all such confiscated properties. At these sales military scrip was receivable in payment, thus enabling those engaged in arms with Walker to seize the estates of those opposing him. Thirdly, a registration law was decreed whereby all land titles and claims were to be recorded within six months. With a frankness worthy of Carrera, Walker tells us that the tendency and object of these decrees were to place the lands of the country into the hands of the white race. But his crowning act of folly, if not insanity, was the decree of September 22d, which was intended to legitimate the institution of slavery.

I have before shown how futile this decree was for any such purpose, because, though reciting the Constitution of 1838, its effect, if such as our Dictator intended, would have been in direct violation of that Constitution, which defines the rights of man to be "Liberty, equality, security of life and property, all of which are inseparable and inalienable, and inherent in the nature of man." Again: "Every man is free, and can neither sell himself nor be sold by others."

But enough of this dreary review of Walker's fatuity and pre-ordained hurdle-race to his own overthrow and destruction.

We may dismiss his political efforts and philosophies by calling attention to the fact that the National Democratic platform of the United States, adopted at Cincinnati June 2d, 1856, contains a resolution drawn, it is said, by Hon. Pierre Soulé, which is worthy of notice, and which Walker intimates was intended as an endorsement of his career. But when we remember that he was in reality the enemy of the Inter-oceanic Canal, we may honor the just and patriotic sentiments of Soulé, while we deprecate the insincerity of Walker. It is pleasant to reflect that amidst the unseasoned and worm-eaten lumber introduced into recent party platforms, the Democratic party of the United States has again expressed its desire in its platform adopted at Chicago on the 22d of June, 1892, for the completion of this the most important enterprise of modern times.

On the 12th of September, Walker had under him about 800 effective men. The First Rifles, numbering about 200, were at Granada; the Second Rifles, under Colonel McDonald, were at Tipitapa, a small town twenty miles northwest of Granada, on Lake Managua. Small detachments were at Masaya and Managua respectively, and two companies of infantry, under Colonel Rudler, were guarding the San Juan river. On the 14th of September a detachment, under Lieutenant-Colonel Byron Cole, assaulted a country villa, or hacienda, called San Jacinto, a few miles north of Tipitapa. Cole, who was one of the originators of Walker's invasion, was unfortunately killed and his party defeated.

About the same time General Belloso, commanding the allied forces, left Leon at the head of about 1,800 men, and commenced his march upon Granada. Walker's detachments, stationed along the route at Masaya and Managua, fell back toward Granada. At Nindiri, three miles from Masaya, Belloso was joined by General Martinez with a reinforcement of 400 or 500 native Nicaraguan recruits, gathered from the Northern Department.

The fighting was now about to recommence in earnest. About the 1st of October, Walker received new accessions to his forces from California and other parts amounting to 175 men, also four hundred minie rifles and two mountain howitzers—a most useful weapon in a country without railway transportation.

Walker, following his usual tactics of assailing the enemy, marched upon Masaya with 800 men, leaving Colonel Fry with 200 reserves in Granada. On the 10th of October the American general attacked General Belloso in Masaya. The San Salvadorian withdrew all of his forces into the main Plaza and the houses immediately around it. The Americans occupied the Plazueta of San Sebastian, and commenced cutting their way through the adobe houses to the Plaza. When darkness set in they had made such progress under the lead of Captain Schwartz of the artillery, supported by Captain McChesney of the Rifles, and Dreux of the Infantry, that the tier of houses fronting on the Plaza alone separated them from the enemy.

What would have been the result of the next day's operations when the opposing forces were brought face to face on the Plaza will ever remain obscured in conjecture, for the reason that startling intelligence now recalled Walker to the relief of his own capital.

General Paredes, being sick at Leon, General Zavala was in command of the Guatamalan troops at Diriomo, a small village about fifteen miles south of Granada. Upon learning Walker's movements, Zavala marched at once upon Granada, and had been assailing the city vigorously before the news reached Walker. Immediately on hearing it, Walker early on the morning of October 13th put his force in motion and attacked the enemy on the Jaltera of Granada, where he had barricaded himself. The garrison, only 200 strong, commanded by Colonel Fry, were inclosed in the Plaza, where they were gallantly defending themselves.

When Walker came up the fight was sharp and decisive. They Guatamalans were put to rout with the loss of two pieces of artillery, and many men killed, wounded, and captured.

The Guatamalans had behaved with great brutality, and Walker complains bitterly of the soldiery, "which an unlettered savage had let loose on the plains of Nicaragua."

It may not be unjust, however, to reflect that this "unlettered savage" (Carrera) was fighting for the existence, independence or supremacy of his native race, which Walker proposed to reduce to slavery.

During the operations around Masaya, Colonel Laine, a gallant Cuban, aid to the General-in-Chief, was taken prisoner and shot. If, however, the allies supposed they could monopolize the business of shooting, they mistook their man. Walker retaliated promptly by shooting a Guatamalan officer of equal rank, and also a captain—the latter thrown in by way of good measure.

Up to this date, say the middle of October, the allies had nothing to boast of in their unequal conflict with the filibusters. They were still in possession of Masaya, it is true, but they had been routed with frightful loss at Granada.

Just here we may remark that whenever Walker

RUINS OF AN ANCIENT CHURCH, GRANADA.

was present on the field with his men, they behaved with gallantry and spirit, and if not always victorious were never thrown into confusion or demoralization. We may justly claim for him, therefore, one essential quality of the successful general—the faculty of inspiring confidence. Among his subordinates, many of whom were as gallant spirits as ever illustrated war, there seems to have been but one officer equal to an independent command. That officer is now about to step upon the theatre of the war in Nicaragua, made memorable by the achievements and ruins with which his name is inseparably connected.

A few days after the battle of the 13th of October, Colonel C. F. Henningsen arrived from New York in charge of arms and ordnance stores for Walker. The latter almost immediately conferred upon Henningsen the rank of Brigadier-General.

The age of adventure in America is over. We have heard with our ears and our fathers have told us of the achievements of such adventurers as Sir Walter Raleigh and Captain John Smith, governor of Virginia, and sometime admiral of New England. Had Henningsen lived in that era, he might have achieved a similar renown. Born in England, in an age of steam and order, he had fought with the Carlists in Spain, assisted Kossuth and his Hungarians, and is now now an American filibuster.

Later on he joined the Army of Northern Virginia, that superb array of soldiery of which the universe will never cease to discourse.

General Henningsen at once set about organizing the artillery and instructing the infantry in the use of the minie rifle.

On November 2d, General Hornsby was sent from Granada to Virgin Bay with 175 men to protect the Transit. Subsequently, he was reinforced by Sanders with 150 rifles, and a howitzer under Captain Dulany, his effective force being on the 10th of November 250 men. General José M. Cañas, commanding the vanguard of the Costa Rican army, was threatening the Transit. Hornsby made a movement against Cañas near Virgin Bay, but the attack (as usually the case, Walker being absent) was unsuccessful. Thereupon, on the 11th of November, Walker, at the head of 250 men, repaired to Virgin Bay, taking with him Henningsen, a howitzer, a mortar, and a squad of sappers and miners. Walker, with that celerity of movement which was his cardinal virtue as a military man, reached Virgin Bay on November 11th, in the afternoon, and at daybreak the next morning assaulted Cañas (commanding 800 Costa Ricans) so furiously that he was compelled to retreat in great disorder. He was driven through San Juan del Sur across the river, up the coast-trail to Rivas, where Walker left him behind his barricades defeated and demoralized.

Walker had been diverted from his former attack upon Belloso, at Masaya, by Zavala's counter-attack on Granada. He seems to have been very anxious to repeat the experiment against Masaya since he now had the assistance of Henningsen and a much more effective artillery corps, which Henningsen and Major Swingle had organized.

The troops were re-embarked, therefore, at Virgin Bay, except Colonel Markham with the First Rifles, who was left at the latter point.

On the morning of the 15th of November, the Americans, 550 strong, were again on the march from Granada upon Masaya.

Before half the distance was accomplished, however, information was received that Jerez had marched to join Cañas at Rivas with 700 or 800 men. To meet this new danger to the Transit, General Walker ordered Colonel Jacques back to Granada with his infantry, there to re-embark for Virgin Bay. Reduced now to less than 300 men, the attack on Masaya, one would suppose, would be abandoned. No good result could be derived from such an attack unless the defeat of the enemy should be so decisive as to drive him back to Leon and relieve Granada from the threatened environment. Such a decisive defeat or route under the circumstances would seem chimerical.

Nevertheless, our General's mania for assailing fortified towns with an inferior force impelled him forward, and, accordingly, on the 16th of November, the enemy's pickets were driven in and a furious assault made upon Masaya. The Rangers were led to the attack by Waters, and the Rifles by Sanders, while Henningsen poured into the enemy a most destructive rain of cannister and round shot, until the Allies were driven from the suburbs into the main town, and the Americans took possession of the high ground which the former had abandoned. This victory of November 15th, indecisive as it was, was dearly purchased at a cost to Walker of one-third of his command in killed and wounded, including some valuable officers. Lieutenant Stahl was killed, and Swartz, Eubanks and West wounded. The attack was continued on the 16th and 17th, until dark of the latter day. The Americans had succeeded in driving the Allies into the Plaza, and were within twenty-five or thirty yards of the houses which were held by the enemy.

At midnight of the 17th of November, Walker, concluding that more time would be required to dislodge his adversary than he could well spare, and his little force being much exhausted, resolved to retire to Granada preparatory to abandoning the Occidental Department. The retreat was orderly and unmolested, and on the 18th Walker re-entered Granada.

CHAPTER V.
1857.

ABANDONMENT OF THE OCCIDENT—DEFENCE OF THE GUADALUPE—"AQUI FUE GRANADA"—SPENCER ON HIS RAFT—THE TRANSIT CLOSED—THE ALLIES CLOSE AROUND WALKER AT RIVAS—HE SURRENDERS TO CAPTAIN DAVIS OF THE U. S. WAR-SCHOONER, SAINT MARY, MAY 1ST., 1857.

It seems probable that the Allies had been reinforced by a large body of Guatamalans just before the attack of the 15th, and it is certain their number was four or five times as great as that of Walker.

The abandonment of the Occident was from the nature of the case, the last act in the drama of filibusterism in Nicaragua. It is only to be regretted that Walker gave to it such a tragical prologue as the wanton burning of Granada.

Twelve months before he had condemned to death two citizens who burned an empty barrack in a small town for fear he might be suspected of having connived at the act. Now he has become so thoroughly Central Americanized that he deliberately devotes to destruction an ancient and beautiful city of 10,000 inhabitants, with no conceivable motive except vandalism, born of defeat, exasperation and revenge.

The work of burning Granada was intrusted to

General Henningsen, left behind for that purpose, while the general-in-chief repaired in person to Virgin Bay, having first sent away his sick and wounded to Omotepec Island, in lake Nicaragua.

Perhaps the most gifted officer in Walker's service was Captain Callender Irwine Fayssoux, whom Walker had placed in command of the schooner *Granada*. On the 23d of December, on Lake Nicaragua, this gallant officer engaged the Costa Rican brig, *Once de Abril*. The log of the *Granada* tells the story briefly and graphically: "At six, within four hundred yards of her, she fired round shot and musketry at us. At eight we blew her up. At ten we had taken from the sea her captain and forty men." The brig carried four nine-pounders and 114 men, all of whom were lost, except those whom Fayssoux picked up. His own loss was one killed and eight wounded. To the credit of Walker, it must be stated that he treated these nautical prisoners with the greatest kindness and gave them passports to return to Costa Rica.

Nor did he fail to reward Fayssoux, though in a manner not quite so realistic as was his kindness to the captured sea-farers. "The day after the action with the '*Once de Abril*,' says he, ' Fayssoux was promoted to the rank of captain, and the estate of Rosario, near Rivas, was bestowed on him for the signal services he had rendered the Republic.

Considering that Walker had not yet captured Rivas, his generosity in giving away the estates of Rosario, must have appealed to Fayssoux's sense of humor. Capture and possession in the natural order of events, should precede final disposition.

We now approach one of the most remarkable achievements of what General Henningsen styles *"irregular troops."* The destruction of Granada, intrusted to General Henningsen and his successful retirement therefrom, in the face of an overwhelming force of the enemy, is a passage comparable to the retreat of the 10,000. Fortunately, Henningsen lived to write out a history in daily detail of his retreat, and this publication, now out of print, was delivered by him into my hands, as it originally appeared, with illustrations in the *Golden Prize*, a periodical published in New York.

Henningsen was not a man calculated to be of any service to Walker in any other than a military capacity. He had the simplicity of a child, with the courage of a veteran. His whole nature was an expression of military adventure, and he knew nothing of affairs.

In the military code he recognized that there was but one phrase—"Obedience to orders." Although his name is generally connected with the destruction of Granada, and although unpeopled structures would proclaim to travelers the barbarism of their destroyer, yet, in reality, Henningsen was the instrument, not the projector; the torch, not the incendiary.

The naked cathedral walls of Leon * respond to

---

* For a description of the ruins of Leon, see II. Stevens, 22.

those of Granada, and ruins answer unto ruins. Central America is herself responsible for her own destruction and desolation. Walker was only a convert to the customs of the country; and although a filibuster, yet he became a Central American. His naturalization was not formal only, but real.

At three o'clock in the afternoon of the 24th of November, the Allies attacked the city at three points. Exclusive of officers and citizens, Henningsen's fighting men reported fit for duty amounted to about one hundred of all arms. Among native soldiery, however, raised by forced levy and mostly Indians, there can be no doubt that artillery, so terribly destructive at close range, inspired a wholesome dread, otherwise it would be inconceivable why Henningsen's little force was not swept out of existence by the simultaneous attacks.

The main part of the town was now in ruins, being destroyed down to the Plaza, where the Americans were concentrated. The fighting on the 24th was closed by a memorable charge of Colonel Neale (whose brother had been killed earlier in the day), at the head of thirty-two picked riflemen, against four or five hundred of the Allies. Neale plunged into their midst with his riflemen, shooting right and left with revolvers, putting them to flight and leaving over one hundred of them killed and wounded on the field. Henningsen says he counted sixteen dead bodies in a spot not forty-five feet square, where the first rifle volley was fired.

On the **25th**, Henningsen **ascertained his force to** be 257 strong *, **encumbered by** seventy-three wounded and sick, and **seventy** women and children. **Of his** original force twenty-seven were cut off at the wharf, which was **about** four **hundred yards from** the **Plaza,** between which and the wharf the enemy had seized two churches, thus intervening **between** the American and his point of embarkation. **He** had sixty horses, and flour **for seven days' rations;** also six pieces of artillery, but only a limited **and wholly insufficient supply of** ammunition.

The little detachment, cut off at the wharf, defended itself gallantly for some days until a **deserter, informing** the enemy of the smallness of their numbers, they were set upon **and after some** loss compelled **to** surrender.

Henningsen **had destroyed all** the houses of the **town except** those **immediately around** the **Plaza,** and nothing remained **but to** burn these and embark his troops. **But** as the enemy had seized two churches which commanded **his route to the** Lake, there was necessity **to** dislodge them.

Henningsen managed **to let a** large **supply of brandy fall** into **the** hands **of the** attacking party, and it is said the **roar of** their carousals rose above that of the fire-arms and artillery.

On the 28th, under flag of truce, the Allies sent a communication addressed "To the Commander-in-

---

* Walker inadvertently states this **as 227.**

Chief of the remains of Walker's forces," signed by Generals Paredes and Zavala of the Guatamalan, General Martinez of the Nicaraguan, and General Belloso of Salvador and Nicaraguan forces, inviting surrender and promising protection and passports to leave the country. To this Henningsen replied in an answer, decided in its refusal, defiant and insulting in its terms. The truth is, he had confident expectation of effecting his escape, and on the other hand had no confidence in this promise of protection in case he surrendered.

To add to the difficulties already surrounding the American General and his devoted little band, pestilence, in the form of cholera and typhus broke out in his entrenched camp. Henningsen, however, made the same discovery that Walker had before observed, namely, that the natives were much more susceptible to disease than the Americans. Hence the Allies suffered more than their adversaries, one of their best commanders, General Paredes, being carried off by the cholera.

In the meantime, during the sixteen or seventeen days that Henningsen had been beleagured amid the ashes of Walker's burnt capital, where was Walker himself? Not idle, we may be sure.

The filibuster general seemed to understand from the outset that he was engaged in a desperate enterprise. But the ring of rifles on the Plaza which would have haunted the imagination of an ordinary adventurer, never seemed to disturb Walker or hasten his movements. He was, as a modern author remarks, "A belated Cortez"—born out of season.*

At Rivas, on the 11th of April, 1856, he deliberately put his back against the lake, with his front to the enemy, so that retreat being impossible, the gage was for victory or annihilation. He took his time about relieving Henningsen, steaming about on the lake daily to see that his flag was still floating in the beleaguered city, but organizing at the same time for defence in the Meridion. When the moment had arrived to relieve the little garrison, he lands Colonel Waters, with 175 Rangers, on the coast a few miles above Granada, and steams away across the lake. This was the burning of the Spanish ships, by which he, in effect, said to Waters, cut your way through to Granada or be obliterated. Waters, the hero of so many fights, understood the alternative.

Between eleven o'clock and midnight of the 12th of January, 1857, Henningsen heard in the distance along the northern coast a fire of musketry, which was immediately answered by the well-known sound of the American rifles. Only those who have listened to the peals of a not distant battle can appreciate the feelings of the devoted little band of filibusters, when they heard the inspiring music of these sharp and dangerously angry rifles. Neither was their clangor a vain noise, for in due season the gallant Colonel Waters, having carried four barricades against immense odds, entered Granada, and

---

* Ford's Tropical America, 372.

with 155 men, of whom thirty were wounded, joined Henningsen.

Henningsen's force now numbered 200 good fighting men, and the Allies despairing of being able to hold the wharf, set fire to and abandoned it. The day of deliverance for the little army was at hand. The Allies, apparently disheartened, and with a wholesome dread of the improvised round shot and cannister, made no serious effort to disturb the embarkation until all were safely on board the *Virgin*. General Henningsen fired a parting shot with his own hand from the window of the Guadalupe Cathedral. On abandoning Fort Henry he stuck up a lance with the inscription: *Aqui fue Granada—(Here stood Granada.)*

Whatever we may think of the act as an act of war, we can but concur with Henningsen's report that as a military achievement the defence of and successful retreat from Granada has few parallels in the history of "irregular armies."

Henningsen estimates that first and last the Allies brought to bear against him a force of not less than 4,000 men. Their loss in killed and wounded was over 800; this does not include those who died of typhus and cholera.

Against this force Henningsen held out from the 24th of November, 1856, to the 11th of January, 1857. The total force under his command when he was surprised on November 24th (1856), numbered 419, of whom 110 were killed or wounded, 120 died

MARKET PLACE, GRANADA.

of disease, cholera and fever, nearly forty deserted, and two were made prisoners. Out of the original 419, therefore, only 166 embarked on the *Virgin*; while of the force brought in by Colonel Waters on the 12th of January, 1857, fourteen were killed and thirty wounded out of 175. And so ended the siege, defence and destruction of Granada. The vacant Plaza, the roofless Esquipulas and the ruined Guadalupe are there still, almost as Henningsen left them.*

The inhabitants returned in due time, but prosperity and peace—these were still in exile. The population of Granada, according to the figures of the " Bureau of American Republics," is 15,000, about what it was when Henningsen commenced its destruction in November, 1856.

The American artillery had instilled a wholesome dread in the minds of the Allied soldiery, and when it was learned that Henningsen was relieved and had joined Walker and that the latter was on his way to the Meridional Department, the enemy abandoned that department and marched northward to join Belloso at Masaya. On December 11th, 1856, Walker had again taken possession of Rivas.

After the burning of Granada nothing but misfortune seemed to pursue the steps of our dictator on Nicaraguan soil. One Spencer, an American, had espoused the cause of Costa Rica, and undertook to place General José Joaquin Mora, brother to the

---
* Ford's Tropical America, 1893, p. 372.

President Don Rafael Mora, in possession of the Transit route, and all the company's steamers on the San Juan, and in the port of San Juan del Norte.

This ingenious and daring American did more to bring the Nicaraguan war to a speedy close than Mora. Belloso, Zavala, or Martinez, or all of them combined, I have already shown the vital importance to Walker of holding the Transit and keeping open the Interoceanic communication. This closed, and the artery which fed the heart of Walker's enterprise would cease to supply life to his adventure.

I have before remarked that Walker had not a single subordiate except Henningsen (and since his gallant march to relieve Granada, I suppose I should except Colonel Waters) equal to a separate command. The same old story of defeat, disaster, surprise, and incompetency has repeated itself from the day when poor Byron Cole fell before a cattle hacienda, near Tipitapa (San Jacinto), to Schlessinger's disgrace at Santa Rosa; and now we approach Lockridge's dissolution of any army of 500 men in the face of the enemy on the San Juan.

The officer whom Walker assigned to guard the Transit, near the mouth of the Serapini, was one Colonel Thompson. Spencer marched from the capital of Costa Rica, San José, to a point on the river San Carlos, and thence floated his men, about 120 in number, down to the mouth of the Serapini. There he fell upon Thompson, who separated from his arms, and without a sentry posted was quietly eating his dinner. Most of his men were killed or wounded, and the remainder captured. This was the first reward of Spencer's genius, acting upon the incompetency of Walker's subordinates.

An effort has been made to produce the impression that Walker's ranks were recruited mainly from the Southern States. No conception could be more erroneous. Among his officers many were English and German, such as Henningsen, Doubleday, Schwartz, and Swingle. Still more were northern, such as the gallant Anderson, the feeble Lockridge, Dolan, and many others. Two States supplied beyond question the majority of his private recruits—New York and California. These were both free States. His filibusters were literally, as the poet tells us, *

"Blown from the four parts of the earth."

Lockridge, as I have stated, was a New York man, and perhaps as capable of command as many other civilians. But we must not forget two facts: First, war is a science, and the average civilian at the head of an independent command is like a ploughman at the helm of a ship; secondly, military academies may instruct captains, but they cannot make them; the great commander is born. The point of what I have written above is this, that Spencer was a born achiever of events, while Lockridge was a born failure. The former, in command of 125 men, proceeded

---

* Joachin Miller.

from one victory to another, until he had not only control of the whole Transit from San Juan del Norte to San Carlos, but had also captured both of the lake steamers, *La Virgen* and *San Carlos*.

These events were like the ticking of the clock of Walker's doom. He looks around in every direction for relief, but finds none. He thinks the English naval commander at San Juan ought to have protected the Transit steamers. He censures the United States for having no war-ship there.

But why should the United States protect property which Nicaragua, acting under Walker's dictation, had confiscated.

The Costa Ricans, through the genius of the American, Spencer, are now in possession of the San Juan, from San Carlos to the Caribbean Sea, and have captured the two steamers which have hitherto conducted Walker to all of his chief victories—La Virgen and San Carlos. Thus the physical impossibility of being in two or three places at the same time has reduced our adventurer to very sore straits.

The interest excited in the United States by Walker's partial successes began to enlist a considerable amount of sympathy. The spirit of adventure was rife; and but for the unfortunate loss of the *Transit*, it is probable reinforcements would have been forwarded in such numbers as to enable Walker to hold his own, and eventually drive the Allies off the soil of Nicaragua.

In the month of January some 240 men reached

San Juan del Norte intended as recruits for Walker's army. Colonel Lockridge was selected by the agent of the owners of the lake and river steamers to regain possession of their property from the Costa Ricans. Lockridge fitted up an old disused river steamer at San Juan, and taking command of the new recruits about the last of January, moved his force up the river to a point several miles below the mouth of the Serapini. On the 4th of February, Colonel H. T. Titus arrived from New Orleans at San Juan with 180 more men. Thus, within one month, 420 volunteers for the filibusters had reached the Republic. On the morning of the 13th of February Colonel Lockridge, having divided his force into two commands, one under Colonel Anderson and the other under Colonel Titus, attacked the Costa Ricans at the mouth of the Serapini and drove them away, and took possession of the position on both sides of the river. The next day Titus, with about 140 men, ascended the river with a view of attacking Castillo. Anderson was left in command at Hipp's Point.

Titus found Castillo garrisoned with a very small force; instead of taking it at once, he began parleying until reinforcements arrived for the Costa Ricans, when, without waiting to ascertain their numbers, he retreated, or rather incontinently fled. Titus now abandoned his command, and returned to San Juan. He was a coward. Lockridge remained inactive, and his force was much weakened by desertion and sickness. About the middle of March 130 fresh men arrived, mostly from Mobile and Texas. These were of excellent quality and fine fighting material.

Lockridge determined to make another attempt to get possession of Castillo Viejo. He accordingly led his force through a trail to a height overlooking the fort, called Nelson's Hill—so named after the great Englishman, Lord Nelson, who in 1780 captured the fort from the Spanish. But the officer now leading the attacking party was not a Nelson by any means. On the contrary, he did not like the appearance of the fortified camp, and retired without any effort to storm it. This may have been wise and prudent, but the result was the abandonment of the effort to clear the river or reach Walker; and immediately thereafter the disbanding of Lockridge's whole force of four or five hundred men. When these discharged men reached San Juan del Norte, the English naval force there stationed was only too willing to assist them in leaving the country. Thus ended the last scene of filibusterism on the Atlantic side of the Republic. Let us now return to the Pacific.

The 500 splendid fighting men which Lockridge disbanded, had they been able through an *open transit* to reach Walker safely in Rivas, would have swollen his forces to over 1,200 men; and with constant increment from the same source no power of the Allies could have driven him out of Nicaragua. The latter, according to Walker's estimate, had dwindled by battle, desertion, and disease from 7,000 to 2,000 during the ten weeks succeeding their advance from

Leon. They were greatly discouraged, and dissensions seemed about to dissolve the Alliance.

But how different the aspect of affairs with General Mora established at Fort San Carlos, the two steamers, Walker's wings, so to speak, tied up by the enemy; and the great "highway of filibusterism" forever closed against its leader! A very short time sufficed to end the war after the middle of March, 1857, and but short space needs to be accorded to its closing incidents. Walker says, sententiously: "The possession of the lake and the river, and the closing of the Transit, gave new life to the leaders of the Allied troops, and they determined to advance into the Meridional Department."

Walker's efforts to break through his investment are only the eagle beating against the wires of his cage.

San Jorge is a pretty little town on the lake shore, only two miles east of Rivas. On the 26th of January, General Cañas, of the Allied army, took possession of this town, and commenced at once throwing up barricades. Walker says that long practice has made the Central American the most expert people in the world in barricading. Cañas was reported to have under him 800 or 1,000 men, and in an almost incredibly short time he had the Plaza of San Jorge and the houses around it strongly fortified. On the morning of the 29th of January, Henningsen, who had been made major-general, accompanied by Sanders, second in command, marched against San Jorge with the First and Second Rifles, Jacques' Infantry, some rangers, a twelve-pound howitzer, and a six-pounder. The first attack on the barricades failed, but nothing discouraged, Henningsen was preparing for a second attack, when the enemy made a sortie, and endeavored to drive the Americans out of some plantain patches they were occupying. But the twelve-pound howitzer again got in its play upon the advancing Allies and drove them back with slaughter. Henningsen availing himself of the enemy's repulse made a second assault upon the barricades, but with worse success than before, because the gallant Colonel Jacques was wounded and other brave officers were killed or wounded.

The loss of the enemy was supposed to be large, but, nevertheless, he remained in possession of San Jorge.

Walker now gave the Allies an opportunity to meet him in the open field by marching to San Juan del Sur with 250 of his men and a howitzer. But the Allies declined the challenge with thanks.

On the 4th of February, not long after midnight of the 3d, Walker, with 200 picked riflemen, marched against San Jorge, and surprised Cañas at four o'clock in the morning. But he met with no better success than had his lieutenants, for he was not only repulsed, but lost some of his best officers, including the valiant and chivalrous Colonel O'Neal, a boy in years, but a veteran in courage and a knight in chivalrous bearing.

Walker now begins to complain of "the fearful epidemic of desertion" which set in and carried off his soldiers by squads, sometimes as many as twenty in twenty-four hours. He seems to think this a strange phenomenon, but when we reflect upon the prospect which looked his command in the face, of early capture and certain execution, after the Central American custom, we can well understand that many would avail themselves of the inducements held out by General Mora in sundry pronunciamentos to the effect that all who abandoned Walker should have safe escort out of the country.

During the month of March, up to the 16th, no battle occurred of any importance, although there were sundry small skirmishes in several of which, according to Walker (a wonderfully frank man), the Allies worsted the filibusters, even when the terms were nearly equal.

On ths 16th of March, the last engagement occurred in which the Americans were the aggressors. It will be remembered that when Walker attacked Masaya in October, 1856, his success was foiled by a counter movement made by Zavala upon Granada. So, on this 16th of March, General Walker's vigorous attack on San Jorge, though apparently successful, only resulted in precipitating the Allies upon Rivas, where Walker was hemmed in, San Juan del Sur having already fallen into the possession of the Allies. The force of the latter in San Jorge, on the 10th of March, had been swelled to over 2,000 men.

Walker attacked the village with 400 troops, two iron six-pounders, one twelve-pound howitzer, and four small mortars. After a hot contest, the Allies could not withstand the artillery which played upon the Plaza, and abandoned that position—and in fact were driven from the village. But in retiring, they took position along the road to Rivas. Now, if Walker's reserve at the latter point had been sufficiently strong to press forward and engage the enemy, the Allied position would have been very uncomfortable, not to say critical. But such was not the case; on the contrary, Walker was hard pressed to regain his own headquarters at Rivas; and soon found himself closely beleaguered there and forced to subsist upon the oxen, horses and mules attached to his command.

There can be no doubt that the Americans did some brilliant fighting upon the 16th, and inflicted heavy loss upon the Allies. Walker lost thirteen killed and sixty-three wounded, four of the latter mortally. The loss of the Allies was put at about 500 in killed and wounded. As usual, when Walker commanded in person, his men behaved splendidly.

As we have seen, the closing of the Transit cut Walker off from all communication with the United States on the Atlantic side, but he was still receiving some small accessions for the Pacific coast from California. Now, however, his friends in the Accessory Transit company, Garrison and Morgan, announce their intention to cease running their steamers altogether. This "treachery," as Walker calls it, was the final and fatal outcome of the ill-advised attack upon Vanderbilt's franchise and property.

Events were now hastening to a close. Left to the equatorial solution, the Allies would now speedily have closed in upon the filibusters, and in spite of their promised protection to all of the Americans except Walker, would no doubt have shot every filibuster, with Central American impartiality. But fortunately, at this critical juncture, there appeared upon the scene just the shadow of the arm of a transcendently great power. *Uncle Sam* stepped in, and, taking his little band of errant filibusters in the hollow of his hand, rescued them from the impending blare of musketry and rifles on the Plaza.

In the afternoon of the 23d of April, General Mora, now in command of the Allied army, under a flag of truce, sent letters to Walker announcing that Lieutenant Huston of the United States vessel, *St. Mary*, was at the headquarters of the Allies, and was ready, under the United States flag, to conduct the women and children in Rivas to San Juan del Sur. Huston remained in Rivas that night, and on the 24th of April conducted the non-combatants to *San Juan del Sur*, under the American flag.

The *St. Mary* was commanded by Captain Charles H. Davis. The gallant Fayssoux was in the port of *San Juan del Sur*, with the *Granada*, and his guns commanded the town.

On the 30th (April) Captain Davis sent, by an aid-de-camp of General **Mora, a** letter to **Walker** proposing that he should **surrender and** go aboard the *St. Mary* to **Panama, Davis to** guarantee his personal safety, **in other words,** "should abandon the enterprise **and leave the** country."

Thus, through the intervention of **Davis,** Walker sent Henningsen **and Waters** to the Allied camp under safe conduct from General Mora, and there the outline of an agreement was reached in a proposition from **Davis to** Walker—the Allies not being anywhere alluded to or mentioned as parties to the same. When, **on the** 1st of May, Henningsen presented **to Walker his report** embodying this proposition, **Walker's** keen eye at once discovered an omission. The proposition, while it made ample provision for the filibusters themselves, said nothing of dispositions in favor of the native Nicaraguans, mostly Leonese, who still adhered to Walker's cause. The poet of the Sierras, describing Walker says that he was " **gentle as a panther,"** and **we have u**ndoubtedly found **him stern** and implacable. But, on the other hand, **simple** justice to his character impels the belief that he would **have** perished **utterly** rather than have deserted or abandoned those who were identified with his cause or had adhered to his fortunes.

He promptly informed Henningsen that he would sign **nothing, and agree to** nothing which did not contain **ample** guarantees for the security both in person and property of the native Nicaraguans, then in **Rivas.** Such a provision was accordingly inserted,

GARDEN SCENE IN GRANADA.

and the final convention contains a "guarantee that all natives of Nicaragua or of Central America, now in Rivas, and surrendered to the protection of Captain Davis, shall be allowed to reside in Nicaragua, and be protected in life and property."

This point being gained by Walker, the details of his surrender were easily made out. Henningsen probably formulated them, for we are told that the convention was "submitted to Davis and signed by him."

General, not President, be it observed, William Walker, with sixteen officers of his staff, were to march out of Rivas with side-arms, personal baggage, etc., and to embark on the United States vessel-of-war *St. Mary's*, in the harbor of San Juan del Sur, to be thence safely transported to Panama.

The privates and other officers, commissioned and non-commissioned, citizens and employees of departpartments, wounded and unwounded, were to be placed under Davis's protection with guarantee of safe and free transportation to Panama.

Such was the "convention" between General Walker and Captain Davis. Upon the whole, every one should have been satisfied because none had a right to complain. With scrupulous accuracy, characteristic of a fearless nature incapable of an intentional deception, Walker gives us his entire force when the capitulation occurred. Of men fit for duty, he had but 274 ; while he was encumbered with 173 sick, wounded and hospital attendants; also 102 prisoners.

Upon the other hand, the Allied army, composed largely of enforçados—enforced men or conscripts—would have suffered a comparatively enormous loss of life before they could have crushed the little band of filibusters, armed with such fatal rifles, and wont to deal out such destructive volleys of grape and canister upon a foe unaccustomed to improved instruments of war. The Allies were only too glad to get rid of these people without being compelled to pay such a costly price for the pleasure of shooting them.

Fayssoux, whose name I can never mention without a thrill of admiration, continued even to the end to bear himself as would become a Paul Jones, a Porter, or a Semmes. He surrendered his vessel, not to the Allies, but to the United States.

CHAPTER VI.

1860.

WALKER MAKES ANOTHER ATTEMPT AGAINST NICARAGUA. IS ARRESTED AND BROUGHT BACK BY COMMODORE PAULDING, OF U. S. NAVY—IS TRIED FOR A VIOLATION OF AMERICAN NEUTRALITY LAWS AND ACQUITTED—HIS DESCENT WITH NINETY FOLLOWERS UPON TRUXILLO, AUGUST 6TH, 1860, IN HONDURAS—HIS SURRENDER TO CAPTAIN SALMON, OF THE BRITISH SHIP "ICARUS"—IS DELIVERED OVER TO THE HONDURANS, AND CONDEMNED TO DEATH BY GENERAL DON MARIANO ALVAREZ—HIS DEATH ON THE FATAL "CAUQUETE"—BURIED IN THE CAMPO SANTO OF TRUXILLO—THE GREATEST AND BEST OF OUR AMERICAN FILIBUSTERS.

WE come now to the closing chapter in the singularly checkered career of General William Walker, the "grey-eyed man of destiny."

And in regard to his aims and achievements, we may as well at this point proceed to dispel several popular illusions entertained both in this country and in Central America.

The first is that he designed, if possible, to annex Nicaragua to the United States. Nothing was farther from his intentions, as is made most manifest by his own declarations and admissions. He over and over

distinctly repudiates any such design or intention.*
His aims were much more lofty and ambitious. He
was going to establish an independent empire, with
himself as chief, based, as we have seen, upon the institution of slavery—not African, but Indian.

A second error, industriously circulated, is, that
the government of the United States, in some manner, or to some extent encouraged Walker in his filibustering enterprises. This supposition is also without the slightest shadow of foundation.† In point
of fact, the Federal Government strained a point in
the opposite direction, and Walker complains bitterly of its failure to recognize him, while England
was openly and notoriously aiding his enemies by
arms and other munitions of war.

Minister Baker, in his introductory chapter, speaks
of a celebration of the anniversary of Walker's surrender, May 1, 1857, and an oration delivered on that
occasion by Senator Zembrana. I have before me
that oration in the original, and in refutation of the
charge of American secret connivance with General
Walker, I translate the following extract:

"But on arriving at this point, in the current of memory, justice
requires that we should pause an instant; because, much as it may
have been suspected that the North American government of those
times looked with great sympathy upon the efforts and success of
the bold adventurer, it must be remembered that its official proceedings were of scrupulous correctness."

---

* See the war in Nicaragua—266, 267.

† The imputation is an insult to history, and an impeachment of that exalted standard of international justice which this nation has ever maintained.

In the third place, I have already exploded the idea that Walker's army was recruited mainly from the population of the Southern States of North America. I have shown that they were soldiers of fortune—adventurers—drawn from every quarter of the globe—

"The cankers of a long peace and a calm world."

This view is likewise confirmed by Senator Zambrana, when he describes Walker's followers as "the scum of the world."

Having corrected these prevalent fallacies, errors, mistakes, in regard to General Walker's aims and his connection with history and the United States, let us follow his declining fortunes to their pathetic, heartrending close.

Walker, unfortunately, in addition to his failure to make the most of the opportunity which fortune had offered him, failed likewise to recognize the truth that a great opportunity once lost is lost forever. "Wreck and ruin," says the philosopher, "if thou have dared when the occasion was not thine." And so our hero eventually discovered. His career, after his deportation from Nicaragua in May, 1857, was a series of petty annoyances and unfortunate mishaps.

He announces boldly and openly that he does not mean to abandon the "regeneration" of Nicaragua. "By the bones of the mouldering dead at Masaya, at Rivas, and at Granada," he exclaims to his comrades, "I adjure you never to abandon the cause of

Nicaragua. Let it be your waking and your sleeping thought to devise means for a return to the land whence we were unjustly brought. And if we be but true to ourselves all will yet end well."

But all did not end well for our unfortunate hero. In November following his capture, he returned to Nicaragua and organized a new force, but Commodore Paulding, of the United States Navy, compelled him to surrender, and carried him with 132 followers back to New York. Under what phase or construction of international law Commodore Paulding acted it is difficult to conceive. Walker had renounced his allegiance to the United States, and become a naturalized citizen of Nicaragua. He was on her territory, engaging in one of her annual or semi-annual revolutions, and was not amenable to any authority but her own. This view was taken by President James Buchanan, one of our profoundest publicists, who refused to recognize Walker as a prisoner of State, and ordered his release. He was tried also in the United States District Court at New Orleans for a violation of our neutrality laws. He was acquitted.

Moreover, it is more than intimated by individuals personally cognizant of those events—original authorities—that after Walker had landed at Greytown and taken Castillo, commercial interests, partly British, no doubt, were appealed to against him. A meeting, said to have been in the interest of the Panama railroad, was held in the office of the American consul, F. W. Rice, and Commodore Paulding, of United

States Navy, being in port, was persuaded to come to Greytown and demand his surrender

Another party on the "*Susan*" Walker not being on board, was wrecked off the coast of Belize, the men taken to Belize, kindly treated and sent home.

Again, in October, 1858, he tried his fortune by organizing a small company in Mobile, Alabama, and setting his face toward the Gulf of Mexico. At the mouth of the Mississippi, however, he was arrested and brought back. He was tried in the United States District Court at New Orleans for a violation of neutrality laws and acquitted.

If, with this verdict in his favor and a record of many hardy and daring adventures, our hero had remained content, it is possible that his genius for war would have found employment in a very short time at home. But a restless spirit or an unrelenting fate impelled him forward to new fields of adventure.

On the 6th day of August, 1860, Walker landed on the eastern coast of Honduras, at Truxillo, and immediately issued his proclamation against the government and called for volunteers to start a revolution. In those countries, unfortunately, a revolution takes the place of a political campaign. The standard of insurrection there is only what we would call a "bolt from the convention." *

As we have heretofore seen, however, the Central Americans are naturally and justly jealous of any

---

* See Ford's Tropical America, p. 385.

foreign interference; and this fact has invested the 1st day of May with a ludicrously exaggerated importance as an anniversary. According to Senator Zambrana—Thermopylæ, Marathon and Salamis must pale their ineffectual fires in presence of the grand result of driving Walker out of Nicaragua.

When Walker landed at Truxillo he had with him about ninety followers, composed of various nationalities, recruited, doubtless, mainly in the United States.

The night of August 6th he disembarked from the three launches, and marching into the town, took possession of the Fort and custom-house. The peaceful inhabitants were panic-stricken, and many fled the town. Walker, as we have said, issued his pronunciamento—without which a Spanish-American revolution would be an opera without music.

It seems that Walker had been in communication with the inhabitants in the island of Ruatan, a Mexican island in the bay of Honduras, and it is said they promised him assistance should he reach there. His aim seems to have been to march through Honduras to Ruatan, and to proceed thence to Nicaragua. Whether or not this was his original intention it certainly became his final ineffectual aim.

Scarcely had Walker time to look around him in Truxillo, when the "*Icarus*," a British vessel, under command of Captain Salmon, of the British Navy, made its appearance in port. The commander at once demanded Walker's surrender to the British, with promise of safe transportation to the United States.

Very naturally, Walker declined with thanks—so much the worse for our intrepid adventurer's fate in the end—but for his fame, so much the better. To but few men is reserved the boon of dying bravely in the sight of history, and in his own sphere the bravest of the filibusters (John Brown not excepted) was Walker.

But the British commander insisted upon his surrender or evacuation. He chose the latter, and on the night of the 21st of August, 1860, he left Truxillo, abandoned his position, not to superior force of Central Americans, but to British dictation.

His idea and intention were to proceed down the coast to the mouth of the Roman river and thence to Swan Island, whence he could open communication with Ruatan, the people of which island had encouraged him, as Walker alleged, to make his last descent upon Central America.

Accordingly, at midnight, on the 21st of August, Walker marched out of Truxillo with eighty-eight men, and proceeded down the coast in the direction of the Roman river. On the morning of the 24th, he had reached a point called Cotton Tree, on the banks of the Roman river and about thirty miles above its mouth. Here he was surprised by a force of Honduran soldiers, but he quickly rallied and formed his little army and repulsed the enemy with his "deadly rifles." While in advance of his troops he himself was wounded in the face, but he quickly brought down his assailant. It is said that the loss of the Hondurans was, out of all proportion, greater than that of the filibusters.

On the night after the battle of Cotton Tree, Walker resumed his march down the river until he reached in safety a place called Limon. Here he was hospitably received and entertained by the Carib Indians, who predominate in the population. On the 27th of August, he reached in safety the Black, or Tonto, river (Rio Negro). Here he encamped, being but two and one-half miles from the sea coast, and remained for three days, resting and recruiting his men. The Hondurans having no navy, Walker felt himself secure from further pursuit, as, undoubtedly, he would have been, but for the entirely unwarranted and unjustifiable interference of the British.

On the 3d of September, two British cutters, carrying forty British marines, and 200 Honduran soldiers, commanded by Captain Salmon of the "*Icarus*," accompanied by General Don Mariano Alvarez commanding the army of Honduras, stepped ashore and demanded an interview with Walker.

It is said there was a strange contrast between the unshaken, quiet, coolness, and dignity of General Walker, and the assurance and bluster of the young British captain of the *Icarus*.

That the authorities of Honduras had a perfect right to capture Walker, and shoot him, too, for that matter, seems too plain for argument. But by what right or title the British interfered and captured our American adventurer is not easily explained, to be perceived or understood. But so it was. Walker would not surrender his sword until he had twice demanded to know if the surrender were made to a British officer, to which inquiry Captain Salmon twice replied, " Yes, you surrender to me as a British officer."

Accordingly, all the arms of the prisoners were delivered up to the British marines, and the filibusters themselves were placed under the guard of these British troops.

On that night while the men were all asleep, General Walker and his second in command, Colonel Rudler, were seized and taken on board the *"Icarus,"* and the next morning (September 4, 1860,) all the prisoners were taken aboard and the British craft weighed anchor, and steamed up to Truxillo, where she arrived that night. On the morning of the 5th, the men of Walker's little army were marched off the ship and paraded in front of 300 Honduran soldiers.

General Walker and Colonel Rudler were then by Captain Salmon formally delivered over to the Honduran authorities, while the remainder of the men were marched away to prison, still under guard of the British marines. Of course, guerilleros and filibusters, and the like adventurers, who engage in private warfare and fight without a flag, cannot expect to be treated according to the usages of war.

Nevertheless, a solemn engagement of a British officer, whereby he secured the surrender of an adventurer who trusted to the religion that blood was thicker than water, it would seem should have been regarded obligatory and imperative.

But such was not the case. Walker and Rudler, after being thus formally delivered over to the Hondurans, were heavily ironed and placed in dark cells, and no one was allowed to communicate with them. Rudler was sentenced to four years of imprisonment. On the 11th of September, the other prisoners were informed by Mr. Squier, an American, that the general was to be shot the next day.

On entering the prison he was immediately placed in heavy irons, and on being asked if he needed anything, replied with a single phrase—"Water."

In his autobiography he informs us that he was of Protestant parentage, but had no hostility towards the Roman Catholic Church. He selected as his ambassador to the United States Father Vigil, a Catholic priest. We find, however, in this same autobiography indications of infidelity. He, in one place, seems to dispute the existence of a personal God by applying the impersonal pronoun "it" to the everlasting and everblessed Supreme Providence.

Upon the fatal *cauquete* (coffin), however, Walker thought differently. He sent for the chaplain of the post (a Catholic, of course), and sought religious consolation.

He died, as his enemies tell us, "full of resigna-

CEMETERY IN GRANADA.

tion." "I am resigned to death," said he to the priest; "my political career is ended."

At eight o'clock on the morning of September 12th, Walker was marched to the place of execution—the Plaza de Armas, the old Square of Arms—and shot.

Alas, for the ring of rifles on the Plaza. It took just ten soldiers to dispatch our brave adventurer, nine in rapid succession, and a tenth after the shudder of a short interval. He died instantly.

As for details, we are told he marched to the place of execution with military step, a crucifix in his hand. He looked neither to the right nor the left, intent only on the diapason of those glorious Psalms of David, which the priest who accompanied him never ceased to recite.

As for his last speech before the fatal fusillade, the better account is that he was too hoarse to make himself heard, and requested the priest who attended him to say a few words to the people. The reverend Father was a Honduran, and a Roman Catholic, and what he said, even if correctly reported, which is doubtful, must be regarded as rather the translation of what his confessor thought Walker *ought* to say than a reproduction of what he himself had actually dictated.

We may not doubt from the evidence that he instructed his confessor to say: "I die in the faith of the Roman Catholic Church. I ask merciful treatment for my comrades, as I alone am responsible for this expedition. If the sacrifice of my life can be of any benefit to society, I lay it down with the greatest readiness. I pardon my judges that I may be able to obtain my own pardon in the next world."

Although there was a shout of soldiers at his death, yet we are told by an eye-witness: "The citizens of the town pitied him, and in the whole crowd there was not one glad countenance."

The shout of the soldiers—those soldiers whom he had defeated more than once, and who were indebted to the British for their victim—was heard by his devoted and sorrowing companions, and they knew what it meant.

The Hondurans refused to bury him. A few foreigners, Americans and others, took up the prostrate soldier and bore him to the Campo Santo—the Sacred Camp—in which our brave filibuster—"the grey-eyed man of destiny"—"the greatest of the soldiers of fortune"—now sleeps in his narrow tent "until that day."

Walker died at the age of thirty-six. In person he was slender and of medium height; his movements were rapid and nervous; in manner he was usually undemonstrative, always calm; in repose, a rather handsome, almost clerical face, with regular quiet features, of no particular significance; but when aroused, they were illuminated by an eye like the glint of broken steel.

If the "poet of the Sierras" had given us a sketch of Walker's personal appearance containing more truth and less poetry, he would have conferred a favor upon history. As it is, his photograph of the filibuster, with "presence like a chevalier, half angel and **half Lucifer,"** is pure fiction. He was, **says** General Rivas **(a** native Nicaraguan), "intelligent, very active, temperate, valiant and unshakable in his purposes." **It is with** singular unanimity testified that he was free from those vices which beset his comrades, the adventurers by whom he was attended. He was, **as is** conceded, **kind and** merciful to prisoners of war ; and the character **of the** men by whom he was surrounded, as **well as that** of the adversaries with whom he contended (as has been well observed by one who **knew him well**), certainly plead much in palliation of his despotic and sometimes **cruel dispositions.** One of his surviving followers **says:** "In my youthful **enthusiasm** I thought our chief a hero, and though in after years I learned **to judge his character** more dispassionately, I have no reason to change my general estimate of him. He was probably the greatest of all the soldiers of fortune."

There is no doubt that **he was the greatest and best of** the filibusters.

Lopez, **John Brown,** Maximillian, none of these could compare **with Walker** in military **genius. His** great forte **was** celerity of movement. **Thus, as we** have seen, **on the** 12th **of** October, 1856, **he attacks** Masaya ; on the 14th he returns to the relief of Granada, and routs Zavala ; thence he proceeds to the Meridional Department, **and on** November **the 12th** assails Cañas, commanding a force more than double his own, near Rivas, and routs him with severe loss; on the next day (November 13th) he returns to Virgin's Bay and embarks for Granada, and on the **15th,** with only 300 men, again attacks the Allies behind the barricades of Masaya. Thus, in a little over one month, he fought four pitched battles and covered a territory embracing the defence of two departments.

As Walker was undoubtedly the ablest, so I think we may say with equal truth that he was the best of our American filibusters of his day and generation.

Lopez, the Cuban, at one time united with the Spanish against his own countrymen, and only espoused the cause of liberty after he had lost the patronage of the tyrant.

John Brown differed from Walker in this, that he pointed his pikes against the breasts of his own countrymen. Walker, it is true, proclaimed all of his opponents to be traitors, and their lives and property forfeited to the Republic; but he never promulgated any decree as bloody as that of Maximillian of October 3, 1865; and where, under pretext of military law, Walker shot one opponent or prisoner of State, it is probable that the infamous Austro-Belgian mercenaries of Maximillian, without any pretense of trial whatever, murdered more than an 100.

The Central Americans seem to cherish no hatred of nor bitterness toward Walker; it is possible, therefore, that these natives would conceive no offence should some kind-hearted Americans replace the rough stone that, under the cross of the Sacred Camp of Truxillo, marks the grave of the "grey-eyed man of destiny," with some more enduring and imposing shaft; inscription—

Here lies the bravest, best, and last of the American filibusters!"

The Nicaraguan Canal.

By the courtesy of my distinguished friend, Judge Lucas, I have been asked to write this chapter for his book. My pleasure in complying with his request was to some extent lessened by the knowledge that my official and business engagements would prevent my giving this great question the attention it deserves. The information herein contained is derived from general and official sources, but especially am I indebted to ex-Senator Warner Miller, Senator Morgan, Senator Frye and the late Commodore Maury—four great masters of the subject of the Inter-oceanic canal.

WM. A. MacCorkle.

Executive Chamber,
Charleston, W. Va., December 16, 1895.

The Nicaraguan Canal.

With but few exceptions imperial possessions have resulted from the demands of commerce, rather than from the desire of war. Commerce, not war, has been the real king. The discovery of new worlds and new countries arose from the needs of commerce. The desire to penetrate to the East Indies by an easy and short route, engage in trade and gather there for Europe the glittering gems, the rich spices and soft silks of the East, brought about the discovery of our continent. Its discovery is most pertinent to the questions which I propose to briefly discuss.

Ever since Columbus discovered America, in the minds of all those interested in commerce has dwelt the question of the possibility of crossing the American continent by water. It has been the dream of the rulers and has been thought over and pondered by the great kings of commerce for three hundred years. Even Columbus, flushed with the discovery of the continent, was disappointed when he could not cross over that continent by ship, plunge into unknown seas and reach the shores of India. The swarthy Spaniard, the sturdy Englishman, the vigorous Frenchman, the enterprising German, have all turned their attention to discovering the secret of the

Strait. Columbus, D'Avilla, Balboa, Cortez, Ponce de Leon, and Captain Smith, all were engaged in finding an entrance through which the waters of one sea mingled with the waters of the other. War, the acquisition of slaves, gold and gems, were the occupation of these hardy adventurers, but above all was the imperial mandate to cross over to the other water. The beautiful incident of Pocahontas was occasioned by the attempt of the sturdy Englishman to find a water path across the continent into the Pacific. Even in the twilight of commerce every one with commercial instincts appreciated the importance of this passage way, and unceasing were their attempts to find it. To find a pass was, in the estimation of these navigators, to discover an empire of trade. From the snows of North America to the succeeding snows of South America, through inlet, bay, gulf, and river ranged vessels attempting to find a passage way. The fierce cruelty and savage unrest of the last days of Spanish military and commercial power are brightened with the dying glory of their attempt to find this great artery of commerce. Freighted galleons, with their swarthy commanders and savage crews, panoplied in leather jerkin and iron coat, have been succeeded by the steamship, yet the quest has not ceased. The Strait does not exist, and the great question to-day before a commercial world is, "Can man do what nature has not done, and will it be profitable to do what nature did not see fit to do?"

The world is no longer isolated. As European

populations have become congested, the demands of commerce have become more exacting for new peoples, new trades, and new countries. No longer can a people live within itself. In proportion as a people has become a sea power, just in proportion has its power increased among the nations of the earth.

To-day this is England's power. Therefore a country to be really great must have the quickest access to the nations of the earth. The shifting sands of the Isthmus of Suez, and the backbone of the Corderillas were the last great bars to commercial freedom. One has disappeared and the civilization of this day demands the passing of the other.

As our knowledge of this hemisphere has widened, the attention of the world has been directed to the lowest altitude of the Continental mountains and to the narrowest portion of land between the oceans. The investigations, therefore, have been directed to that part of the continent lying between the Gulf of Campeachy and the Gulf of Tehauntepec, in Central America, and the Gulf of Darien, on the Caribbean Sea. From these investigations three routes for the Inter-oceanic canal, which are at all feasible, have been suggested. They are the Isthmus of Tehauntepec, lying closer to the United States than any other route; the Nicaraguan route, lying within the States of Nicaragua and Costa Rica, and the Panama route, lying within the Republic of Columbia.

No part of the world has been surveyed, re-surveyed, and re-investigated as has been this portion of this hemisphere. Since 1771 there have been made twenty-one surveys of this narrow territory between the oceans. The great question is which route is preferable, which one is the cheapest, and which one, all things considered, will best serve the demands of the world's commerce. Every selfish commercial interest demands that on the question of location the United States should favor the Tehauntepec route. The Isthmus of Tehauntepec will allow the commerce of the United States to pass through the Gulf of Mexico from the Mississippi river into the Pacific Ocean without once having to pass through the straits leading into the Caribbean Sea and the Atlantic Ocean. All the protection needed to commerce during war can be furnished easily by this government within the Gulf of Mexico, and, in times of peace, there would be no necessity for braving the longer voyage and the winds of the Caribbean Sea. This route would be shorter, cheaper, and every strategical and military interest would demand that we seize upon it in preference to any other. The Tehauntepec route is 150 miles in length, with an altitude of 765 feet. This great altitude, the contour of the country, and the want of water at the summit militate against the possibility of successful water transportation over this isthmus. A great engineer presented a scheme of a ship railway by which ships were to be lifted from the waters of the Gulf of Campeachy, placed upon the railroad, dragged across the isthmus in bulk, and placed again in the waters of the Gulf of Tehauntepec, on the Pacific side. Captain Eads, with the great ability which characterized all of his undertakings, impressed the advantages of a ship railway upon the country, and for a time there were people well versed in engineering problems, who believed that the scheme was feasible. In the first place, leaving out the question of the feasibility of this great undertaking, it has been demonstrated that it would not be possible for ships to pay the enormous freight demanded by the vast expenses necessarily entailed upon their passage by railroad. Railroad traffic is from five to ten fold more expensive than water traffic, and the expense of the operation of this road would be enhanced by the stupendous nature of the paraphernalia necessary to carry the great ships of modern times. To-day the plan of the ship railway is dead with the great man who conceived the idea. For all purposes of a ship canal the route of the Isthmus of Tehauntepec has been abandoned by those interested in the canal.

Passing on down to the Republic of Columbia we find the narrowest part of the coast, the isthmus of Panama, forty-seven miles in width with an altitude of 325 feet. This portion of the isthmus has always had a fascination for minds engaged in the construction of the canal, because it is the narrowest portion of land on the hemisphere dividing the two oceans. A sad memory lingers around this narrow neck of land, as being associated with the failure of the great man who attempted to build here the inter-oceanic canal. Narrow, it is true, is the isthmus, but engineering problems are here presented which possibly science may overcome, but not without the expenditure of vast sums of money which would burden ocean traffic more than it could bear. The great engineering problems here are, first, the Chagres rivers, with its great variation of flow; the great Culebra Cut, with its walls of slippery mud; and the want of water at the summit level sufficient to feed the canal. The French company undertook to canalize the Chagres river and crossed that stream no less than twenty-seven times, because they had not studied its character and they wished to keep near the river along which the railroad ran, which last was the base of their supplies. This river drains fourteen hundred square miles, and the volume of water which poured down from the precipitous sides of the high mountains of its water shed could not be controlled by any human agency.

A friend of mine, a former manager of the Panama railroad, and a man of great ability, whose experience with this river is very great, informed me that in twenty-four hours he has seen the Chagres river rise seventy feet, and from a placid stream become a tumultuous mass of water, absolutely uncontrollable by the present engineering science. In his judgment the canal could never be built across the Panama route. It was attempted by De Lesseps to control this river by a great dam, into which the overflow could go, but this was found to be impracticable, as the volume of water in the rainy season was too great. To obviate this difficulty it was proposed to construct a tunnel nine miles through the mountains, and carry off the overflow into another valley. The great canal engineer wedded to his idea of the sea level Suez canal, depressed the bottom of the Panama canal to the sea level. This intensified the terrible power of the torrential Chagres. In addition to all of this, by reason of the tides on the Atlantic coast being only one and three-fourths feet in height, while on the Pacific coast they have raised to nineteen feet, it was seen that locks would be necessary. Here they were met by the same problem as at Tehauntepec. There was no water to supply the summit level. With the ingenuity which characterized this great man, it was proposed to pump water into the summit basin. When it came to the question of supplying water for the transportation of the great ocean steamers of the world by pumping it into the inter-oceanic passage, even the vigor and energy of the French nation wore out and the combat with nature was abandoned.

The other difficulty at Panama was the Culebra Cut, which consists of a cut of sixty million cubic yards of soft, slippery rock, laying in horizontal layers, which will not stand when excavated. If possible this is a more insurmountable difficulty than the Chagres river.

These are the chief engineering objections to Panama, but a greater commercial objection still exists.

The Isthmus of Panama is one of the most unhealthy sections of the world, and it lies at the end of a landlocked bay, through which the trade winds never blow, and the location of the canal at that point would require the towing of a sailing vessel for at least one hundred miles to the mouth of the canal.

The other route which has been considered is the route across Nicaragua. This route is 160 miles in length, with an altitude of 153 feet, as against an altitude of 765 feet at Tehauntepec and 325 feet at Panama.

At first contemplation you are impressed with the fact that the Nicaragua route is more than one hundred miles longer than the Panama route. This seeming disadvantage is compensated by the fact that here there are great natural advantages for this work. By the Nicaragua route there are only twenty-six and one-eighth miles of excavation, while there is free navigation in the lake and river and basins of 142 miles. On this route is the beautiful fresh water Lake of Nicaragua, which, with a little dredging, is deep enough for the largest ships of the world. The San Juan river, which is singularly free from torrential variations, completes the largest part of the remainder of the route. The consensus of opinion of great engineering experts and the reports of the various commissions appointed by this government have all been to the effect that this route is the most feasible one across Central America.

The problems involved in this work are the great-

est which can occupy the human mind. The passions and small affairs of every day life are dwarfed when considering these most interesting questions. To discuss the construction of this canal it is necessary to look not alone into the mere engineering problems, but into all of the questions which necessarily arise from the peculiar nature of the work. All of the great questions which disturb the world inhere in this discussion. The question of diplomacy, of military strategy, of commerce, and of engineering, all here find their highest level, and all have been contemplated in every phase by the nations of the earth.

Even if the writer had the ability it would be impossible within the limits of these few pages to more than briefly discuss the salient points of each one of these great problems. They are all of great interest, and the one which naturally arises for consideration first in the minds of men is the engineering question. From an engineering or constructive standpoint, can the canal be built? Men versed in such matters say that it is feasible.

While the writer has no special knowledge of engineering science, still, from the many surveys and elaborate reports and careful examinations of great engineers, he may briefly and in a general manner discuss the constructive features of the canal.

On this route there are no problems which have not been met by engineering science. Enormous dams are needed, but already larger ones are in use in this country. Great locks are demanded, but there are to-day more capacious ones in the United States. Great masses of rock are required to be removed, but far more stupendous operations in rock work have been carried out in the engineering world. Much dredging is necessary, but on our lakes there has been as much required and successfully completed.

The harbor at Greytown, the Ochoa Dam, and the Great Divide Cut are the three great works confronting engineering science. The first consideration for the engineers is, is there a sufficient and abundant supply of water at the higher levels not subject to great fluctuations of rise and fall? As I have elsewhere shown this want destroys the feasibility of the Panama route.

The central figure of the Nicaraguan canal is the great lake of Nicaragua. This lake furnishes the only solution as to the supply of water on the Central American Isthmus. It is 106 feet above the sea level and furnished daily ten times the amount of water required for the operation of the canal. A great water shed, drained by this lake and Lake Managua, restricts the rise and fall of the San Juan river, its outlet, to a maximum of five feet.

Lake Nicaragua approaches the Pacific on the western side to within twelve and a half miles. By the river San Juan, its outlet towards the Atlantic, it is sixty-four and one-half miles. The lake navigation itself will be fifty-six and a half miles.

The Lake Nicaragua itself is a body of water of 110 miles in length and forty miles in average width, and averages from eighteen to 150 feet in depth. At Fort St. Carlos, the outlet of the lake into San Juan river on its way to the Atlantic, for some miles there will be a large amount of bottom dredging necessary. This is through soft mud and the engineers have reported that it is entirely feasible.

The river San Juan is from 500 to 1,200 feet in width and will be followed by the canal for a distance sixty-four and one-half miles from the lake to the dam, at Ochoa, just above its connection with the Machado river. At this place a great dam will be constructed, which will make the river the same summit level as that of the lake. This will give slack water navigation the whole distance from the Ochoa dam into and across the lake. At this point the San Juan river strikes the lowlands and from Ochoa is tortuous and shallow and will no longer be followed. The canal will be constructed through the valleys of the San Francisco and the Deceado rivers, in which valleys great basins will be formed by large embankments; the sea level being reached by three locks. The east lock on the Atlantic side being nine and one-fourth miles from Greytown, which gives a summit level of $153\frac{1}{4}$ miles out a total distance of $169\frac{1}{2}$ miles.

On the western side the last lock is only three and one-half miles from Brito on the Pacific coast. It will require seventeen and one-fourth miles of canal from the shores of the lake to the port at Brito on the Pacific. Of that distance eleven and forty-four hundredths miles will be wholly in excavation and five and six-tenths miles through the basin of the valleys of the rivers Grand and Tola. On the way to the ocean, the canal will go through a great depression in the valley of the Tola, which by means of a dam, will furnish a basin of water of 4,000 acres with a width of 13,000 feet. There will be three locks upon this side as there are upon the Atlantic side, the greatest of which will be 650 feet long, eighty feet wide and with a lift of forty-five feet. Between the last lock on the Pacific side and Brito, the canal will be used as an enlarged part of the harbor.

In short, the Nicaragua canal will consist of the great basin of the lake, connected with the Atlantic Ocean by the San Juan river, excavated canal work and river basins on the Atlantic side, and excavated canal work and the Tola basin on the side of Pacific.

One of the great problems is the harbor at Greytown. This was formerly a good harbor, but for many years has been closed by a bar, but the Maritime Canal Company has re-opened this harbor by the building of a jetty across the bar for the space of 1,000 feet. This will be extended for a distance of 1,700 feet, forming a capacious harbor. This jetty has already made a permanent depth of ten feet in the harbor, which will be increased to a depth of thirty feet by dredging and by the action of the water upon the artificial work. When this is completed the largest vessels will be able to enter the harbor, and it will be capacious enough for all purposes of navigation and safety. The harbor, when excavated, will give a total area of 340 acres of water, twenty-eight feet deep. This has included part of the canal at the first lock.

At Brito, on the Pacific, there is no great question as to the possibility of constructing the harbor. The plan here is to build a breakwater which will extend from a promontory, and nearly opposite to this will be constructed another breakwater. It is believed there will be no trouble in the construction of this harbor.

One of the most stupendous works is at Ochoa, where a dam is constructed, which will raise the river to the level of the lake. This great work will be 1,200 hundred feet in length and seventy feet in height, but, as I have said before, this dam will not be as large as many that are at present in existence. It will not be constructed as rock dams are ordinarily constructed by placing rock carefully on line, and bound by cement, but will consist of a great mass of rock, dumped into the river from a bridge overhead, and these rocks will be allowed to form a natural bed, and will be built in that way to its height. The river full of debris percolating through this rough wall will, in a comparatively short time, fill up the gaps, and will make a dam that no disturbance of the earth will in any wise interfere with.

Vast and extensive weirs will be constructed here so as to take care of the necessary overflow of the water.

In the valley of the Deceado, on the western portion of the canal, there will be another great embankment, seventy feet high and 1,050 feet wide, which will make a basin three miles long with a depth of from thirty to seventy feet. In addition to this great basin on the Atlantic side, and so near to the locks on the eastern side, as well as the Tola basin on the western side, there will be two great basins or reservoirs, where ships can rest and wait and make repairs, and where they can pass each other under full speed without danger to navigation.

The Great Divide Cut on the eastern division will be one of the most stupendous pieces of work of rock cutting that the world has ever seen. It will require the canal to be cut three miles through an average height of rock 140 feet, and a maximum height of 320 feet, and will require the removal of 12,000,000 feet of rock. This rock is in the main solid rock, and is absolutely necessary for the construction of the canal. It will be needed in the great dam at Ochoa, and in the construction of the jetties at Greytown, and in the building of the locks.

The depth of the canal is thirty feet, and the lowest width on the bottom will be 100 feet. There is a total distance from ocean to ocean of $169\frac{1}{4}$ miles, of which there will be free navigation in the lake, river and basins of $142\frac{1}{2}$ miles. The width and depth of the canal with its lakes and wide basins will be a great economy of time, and it will only require twenty-eight hours to pass through, against about thirty-one in the Suez canal. By comparison with the Suez, we find that the latter canal is eighty-eight miles in length, of which there is sixty-six miles cut through the earth in excavation. For eight miles there was no work whatever on the Suez, the natural depressions already existing.

The locks used upon this canal are about the same as that used on the Sault St. Marie canal. Their great size may give no uneasiness as to their ability to do the work required. The lift of forty-five feet is but small as compared with the lift of the lock which is being constructed between Lake Erie and Lake Ontario. This latter lock has a lift of eighty feet, and is said to be entirely feasible. The Nicaragua canal has been constructed upon a plan sufficiently ample to supply the needs of the world's commerce. Profiting by the example of Suez, the original estimates are made large enough to do away with any possibility of an increase in capacity being required for many years to come.

This great work will require a vast amount of money, and no private corporation or person will be able to build it. It is proposed that this government furnish the money, and the plan proposed in the last Congress was that $70,000,000 out of a $100,000,000 in stock should be transferred to the United States, giving the power to this government or its representatives to vote a majority of the shares; the government reserving all power to alter, amend and repeal the charter.

Out of fifteen directors, six were to be appointed by the President of the United States, and if necessary the Secretary of the Treasury could control the other 70,000,000, and thus give the United States a majority of the directors. Five million dollars was to be given to Nicaragua for its concession, and 1,500,000 was to be given to Costa Rica. The Maritime Canal Company was to have the money expended by them repaid and a comparatively small sum for its concession. Costa Rica and Nicaragua were each to have a director. The government of the United States was to guarantee the bonds of the company to the extent of $100,000,000 for the construction of the canal, if that was necessary for the construction, and said bonds were to be delivered upon the certificate of the United States engineers, that work in proportion had been completed. The construction of the canal was to be under the control of the engineering department of the United States Government. It is impossible to see how the government could make a better contract. Upon the lowest estimate of revenue at the time of completion, the government would have a large per cent. upon its investment. It would absolutely control the canal in every sense of the word, and by furnishing the money no private individual can do, it would relieve the commerce of the world of a great burden. If any private corporation attempted to complete it, the work with the interest on the borrowed money would cost $250,000,000. This would be just that increased burden on commerce. From all data it seems that as an engineering question there is no doubt about the feasibility of the enterprise.

Conceding that the building of the canal is possible, and that it will be useful to commerce when completed, the question arises from whence will come its revenue? Will the canal from a commercial standpoint pay? The great bounding vigor of American commerce answers that it will be a commercial success. The success of Suez and of the Sault St. Marie proclaims in terms which cannot be mistaken that a barrier such as this should no longer impede commerce. Let us compare this canal with some similar works. The Sault St. Marie, connecting Lake Superior and Lake Huron, was constructed in 1855. This was for those days a large work with a large lock and with a canal twelve feet in depth, but such has been the vast increase in commerce that the government has here constructed a lock 800 feet long; the largest lock in the world. The commercial world shows nothing like the increase of trade which has been created by this improvement. In 1881 freight passed through the lock in round numbers amounting to a million and three-quarters tons. In 1892 it had increased to eleven and a quarter million tons. In 1894 it had further increased to thirteen million and two hundred thousand tons. Great experts have estimated that this tonnage, if charged for, would have paid in the year 1889 over $40,000,000 of freight. Of this tonnage eighty-five per cent. was coal and iron; and this traffic was actually created by cheapness of water transportation. The tonnage of this canal is in volume of business over thirty-three per cent in voyages and ten per cent. in freight larger than the tonnage of the Suez Canal; and this tonnage is upon inland lakes, whose shores are girdled with competitive railway tracks.

When De Lesseps proposed the cutting of the Suez canal there were men who said that the world's commerce would not bear it; that from a commercial standpoint it would not pay, and that it could not be built. Let us see how their gloomy forebodings jostle with the truth. In 1870 there passed through the Suez canal 486 ships with tonnage of 436,609, and the receipts from tolls amounted in that year to $867,152. In 1888 this had increased to 3,440 ships, with a tonnage of 6,640,834, and the receipts had increased in round numbers to $13,000,000. In 1894 the tonnage had increased to 8,039,105, and in the same year the rate was reduced to one dollar and ninety cents per ton. The Suez Canal cost £20,000,000; the operating expenses last year amounted to $1,000,000. The magnitude of the operations of the Suez cannot be compared with that on the canal of the New World, and the saving of distances will be infinitely greater by the Nicaragua than by the Suez canal. Between London and Canton the Suez saves 3,300 miles, while the Nicaragua canal saves from 5,000 to 8,000 miles on nearly all of the voyages. Between London and San Francisco it saves 7,200 miles out of a voyage of 14,700 miles. Between New York and San Francisco it saves 10,080 miles out of a voyage of 14,840 miles. Between New York and Canton 6,500 miles shorter than Suez and over 5,000 miles shorter than around the Horn.

In almost every case the saving of time and distance by the Nicaragua canal will be largely over that saved by the Suez. In the circumnavigation of the earth by the Suez the distance was reduced two thousand four hundred and thirty-three miles, whilst by the Nicaragua canal the reduction will be six thousand and fifty-four miles. These comparative figures show that from every consideration of time and expense of voyage the great advantage will be with the American canal. The most moderate estimates show traffic at from six to seven million tons for the first year, which at $2.50 per ton would bring fifteen million dollars of revenue per year. Taking off a million and a half dollars for operating expenses, which is a large estimate, we would have six per cent. on two hundred and twenty-five million dollars.

As a matter of fact, the normal amount of freight by the year 1900, before which time the canal cannot be completed, will be about twelve million tons per year, which at one dollar per ton toll will leave, after operating expenses, about eleven million dollars clear income.

For the completion of the canal the estimate of the Maritime Construction Company was sixty-five million eighty-four thousand one hundred and seventy-six dollars; this was increased by the estimate of the board of engineers, to which the question was submitted, to eighty-seven million seven hundred and ninety-nine thousand five hundred and seventy dollars. A fair estimate is generally conceded to be one hundred million. From the report which was made in 1879 to the International Canal Congress at Paris it was estimated that the tonnage existing in 1898 would furnish five million two hundred and fifty thousand of tonnage for the canal. This was a moderate estimate, but accepting it as reasonable and looking into the countries absolutely tributary, as well as those countries largely tributary, it will be seen that traffic of from ten to twelve million tons per year is but a natural and early consequence of the opening of this great work. Consider but a moment the mighty forces at work. The world has never seen any progress such as this Republic shows. Within fifteen years, at the outside, we will have one hundred million of people, and within sixty years from now we will have two hundred million. The movement of freight on the lakes amounted in 1890 to 53,424,432 tons. Think of this; and men to-day are hunting wild deer on the borders of the lakes. By no rule can you estimate the advance and increase of a free people. The convention reasoned from the former increase of commerce that the estimate of five million two hundred and fifty thousand would raise to seven million two and fifty thousand in ten years. This reasoning was predicated upon the advance of the world's commerce previous to that date. As a matter of fact the increase of commerce within the estimated time raised far above this estimate, and for the whole world instead of an expected moderate increase it amounted to the marvelous increase of eighty-eight per cent.

Let us take the traffic of the world, which is absolutely tributary to the American canal. It is about as follows:

The trade of Great Britain with Ecuador, which last year amounted $4,484,013; with Peru, which last year amounted to $6,573,838.00; with Chili and Bolivia, which last year amounted to $38,437,629.00; a total of $49,495,480.00.

The trade of Belgium with Peru, which last year amounted to $6,777,870.

The trade of our Atlantic ports with Hong Kong, which last year amounted to $1,344,474; with China, which last year amounted to $14,778,505; with Japan, which last year amounted to $11,933,693; with British Australasia, which last year amounted to $11,481,910; with the Phillipine Islands, which last year amounted to $3,919,543; with Hawaii Islands, which last year amounted to $613,034; with Chili, which last year amounted to $6,778,562; with Ecuador, which last year amounted to $1,325,417; with Peru, which last year amounted to $9,635,629—a total of $53,138,767.

The trade of all the Pacific ports of the United States with Belgium, $757,684; with France, $766,492; with Germany, $883,566; with Great Britain, $21,702,521; with Cuba, $216,112—a total of $24,323,375.

This above enumerated trade is entirely and absolutely tributary to the canal. This aggregate trade last year amounted to the vast sum of $133,738,492. To this vast commerce there was not added the commerce of the Atlantic and Pacific coasts with each other. This last commerce can scarcely be estimated. The movement of freight by water on the Atlantic and Pacific coasts almost surpasses belief. It amounted in 1890 to 80,817,251 tons. Every interest of the East and West will be more closely linked by this work to the interests of trade that demand an increased reciprocity between these two great sections of our republic. To-day we must understand that the rate for transportation between New York and San Francisco by rail is twenty dollars per ton, and by sailing vessel ten dollars, and that by sail around the Horn the voyage is 120 days. This rate is to-day prohibitory on many articles of commerce, which, if the rate were reduced, would furnish thousands of tons of commerce. See the effect of the shortening of voyage upon our great commerce to Hong Kong and China. This trade last

THE BREAKWATER AT GREYTOWN—LOOKING SEAWARD.

year with the United States amounted $16,122,979. This voyage is about 170 days by sailing vessel; by canal route it would only be 100 days by sail and forty days by steam. The far-reaching fact upon trade can scarcely be estimated. Experts of shipping matters all contend that a large per cent. of return commerce between Great Britain and her Eastern colonies would pass through the Nicaragua canal. This route, with more favoring winds, more temperate climate, more favorable currents, and on the other matters of economy and of time and expense, will demand that a vast deal of this traffic on its return from the East Indies will pass over this canal. In addition to this there is a large amount of the English traffic, which comes by return from the East Indies, which is taken to London and reshipped to the United States. This no longer need be done, and merchandise, such as plumbago from Ceylon and braid from China, will be taken to New York on return trip, unloaded there, and the ship will load again in New York with American products for its trip across the Atlantic. The trade above spoken of is a trade which is absolutely and entirely tributary to the canal. There is a large amount of trade which is largely tributary—that is, the trade of Great Britain—with Hong Kong, $12,-715,788; New South Wales, $78,971,757; Queensland, $22,316,935; South Australia, $22,334,325; Victoria, $53,102,442; Western Australia, $4,746,-921; New Zealand, $58,764,414; Tasmania, $15,791,-

072; Java, $11,342,600; Phillipine and Ladrone islands, $2,471,755; China, $39,619,894, and Japan, $23,703,673.

This trade amounted last year to $347,851,576. The trade of France with Japan, $11,723,000; and Chili, $11,704,000; which together last year, amounted to $23,427,000. The trade of Germany with Australia, $5,622,480, with Japan, $3,605,280, and Chili, $26,439,120, which together last year, amounted to $35,666,880. The trade of our Atlantic ports with the British East Indies, $22,512,327, the French East Indies, $69,136, the Dutch East Indies, $8,757,897, and Central America, $11,989,215; which together last year amounted in all to $43,328,575. This amounts in the aggregate to $450,324,031, and is largely tributary to this canal

The total imports into Great Britain from her East Indian Colonies amounted to $200,000,000, and of this trade, as I have said before, a large amount will seek its way through the canal. A large amount of the traffic of England between Chili, Peru and Bolivia will take its course through the canal from the fact that between Bolivia and Liverpool the canal will shorten the journey 4,090 miles, and between Valparaiso and Liverpool, 2,144 miles. From all of the northern part of Peru unquestionably traffic will be through this canal. Every climatic and natural reason will be in the favor of a great increase even from this estimate. It must be understood that no sailing vessels make their journey through the Suez canal, and that the journey, even in the Mediterranean Sea, is fraught with great difficulties by reason of the almost certain head winds outside of Gibraltar; whereas with the Nicaraguan canal the trade winds blow and the currents are propitious for sail vessels. The increase on the above estimate of tonnage will be appreciated when we consider that in eighteen years the tonnage of the world has increased from 23,000,000,-000 to 63,000,000,000 of tons, and that the commerce of Great Britain, France, Germany and the United States increased from 1879 from 8,014,880,620 tons to 8,890,200,783 tons in 1888, an increase of 875,530,-160 tons, a growth so great that we can scarcely grasp its magnitude. The advantage which the canal will give the United States, with our commercial energy, will be an advantage such only as this one great artery of commerce can furnish. It will develop new methods, new territories, new industries and new modes of transportation. The rapid peopling of our country demands that our productive energies shall no longer be given to the development of internal commerce, but that our attention shall be directed to the world. Our only great competitor in many sections of the world in which she is supreme, will no longer have the advantage which she has had in the past. We will be 7,000 miles nearer western South America than we are to-day, and have the advantage over her of that distance in the markets of that great section.

At the inception of the Suez canal England was

opposed to its construction because she was the greatest sea power and in any naval or commercial conflict concerning her Eastern possessions she could, by reason of her naval superiority, easily distance her rivals. With her wise foresight she had contrived to mark out her way to the East, and had placed her great South African Colonies on the road to India. With the Suez canal completed the route to the East being so much shorter and the Continental powers possessing equal privileges through a neutral canal, England would have no advantage arising from her naval superiority. When, in spite of her opposition, the canal was built, she purchased the stock control of it, seized Egypt and more carefully fortified her Mediterranean islands. From a commercial standpoint, the stock for which she gave $20,000,000, could be sold to-day for a $100,000,000, and from a military standpoint she possesses the key to India and the East.

More than this, the Suez canal has added immeasureably to England's commerce. Her tonnage to the Orient has increased far beyond her tonnage to any other portion the world. This has resulted from the great advantage which the Suez canal has given her. She has three-fourths of the tonnage passing through the canal. In 1883 Great Britain had a gross tonnage of 7,977,728 tons, as against 798,929 of German tonnage and 702,634 of French. Her trade with the East has increased from 537,000,000 in 1870 to 752,000,000 in 1888. This all results from the Suez canal. You must remember that the Nicaraguan canal is right in the midst of the world's commerce, whilst the Suez is only a mere passage-way. The tonnage of America will be largely increased by the Nicaraguan canal. The need of this canal to our commerce is plainly shown by our tonnage. By the map you will see how the Suez canal hurt us. It gave England from three to five thousand miles the advantage of us. In the foreign trade in 1893 our aggregate burthen was 883,199 tons, an actual decrease of nearly one hundred thousand tons from 1892. Of the total foreign trade for 1894 8.7 per cent. was carried in vessels belonging to the United States, whilst of the total tonnage of the world Great Britain, by reason of her commercial foresight and her advantages resulting from the control of the trade avenues, had 13,192,566, as against 2,068,859 of the United States. This should no longer be tolerated by this great and enterprising people, and every agency should be grasped to increase our commerce to the volume which our power as a commercial people deserves.

The saving to the commerce of our country in distance and money is well exemplified by the following table:

From New York to San Francisco it is 14,840 miles by Cape Horn. By the Nicaraguan canal it is 4,946 miles, a saving of 9,894 miles. From New York to Melbourne by Cape Horn it is 13,502 miles. By the canal it is 10,000 miles, a saving of 3,290 miles. From New York to Hong Kong it is 18,180 miles around the Horn; by the Nicaraguan canal it is 11,038 miles, or a saving of 4,163 miles. From New York to Guayaquil it is 11,471 miles around the Horn; through the Nicaraguan canal it is 3,053 miles. The distance saved is 8,418 miles. From New York to Acapulco it is 13,283 miles around the Horn; by the canal it is 2,709 miles, a saving of 10,874 miles on the voyage.

The value of this canal to the commerce of the United States is illustrated by the report of Mr. T. B. Adkins, a great master of the subject of trade, to the Senate committee, where it is shown that a 1,650 ton barque will cost in transportation charges $75 a day, not including port charges. And that on the voyage from Port Townsend to Boston there will be a saving by the canal of about 10,600 miles, which would amount in actual saving of expense to $6,225 in the mere running of the vessel. This is a fair illustration. Transportation is the great question of the world to-day, and in the commercial world the demand for cheap and certain transportation is as urgent and vital as is the demand for a cheap first cost of the articles of commerce. This canal fully answers this request of commerce. Particularly speaking, how will the canal affect our country? What section will most potently feel its effect?

An authority has said that the chief advantages resulting from its construction will be reaped by the Pacific coast. It is true that the benefit to this wonderful section of our Republic will be immense, but these advantages will, in my opinion, scarcely be as great as those which will accrue to the Mississippi valley. Let us examine the three great sections which will be peculiarly benefited by this work, and discuss somewhat in detail the peculiar advantages which will accrue to each section. In the Mississippi valley nature has indeed been prodigal of her bounties. Here is every climate, every product of the temporate regions, and, in addition, here are the utmost facilities for manufacture. Within this great valley nature has located all the great minerals excepting gold and silver. She has made wheat and corn and rye and rice grow in the same valley with the cotton and the hemp. Here are the greatest forests, the greatest mountains of iron, the richest copper mines, sufficient marble to supply the palaces of the earth, and lead enough to furnish the armies of Europe for 500 years.

A great writer has said that coal and iron are the kings of the earth, because they make and unmake the kings of the earth. England's greatness is founded largely upon her coal, but virtually within the valley of the Mississippi, within the great Appalachian chain, there is nine times the coal that is within the bosom of Great Britain. The world is more dependent upon coal and iron and cotton than upon any other articles of commerce. That which increases the production and widens the distribution of these great articles of commerce will exert the greatest influence upon the affairs of the world. We will consider the two great staples of coal and cotton in this valley, and briefly discuss the influence which the building of the canal will have upon them. Great Britain to-day exports 20,000,000 tons of coal and 2,500,000, tons go to South American markets. These markets she now controls. The opening of the canal will almost revolutionize the trade in coal, and will largely revolutionize the trade in cotton, and from this will largely follow the revolution of all trade. The question of fuel is most important, and the discussion of the effect of the canal upon the coal trade is directly in point.

The coals which supply the Pacific coast come almost exclusively from British possessions. The best of the Pacific coast coals come from Vancouver, and they are the only known coals on the Western coast which are good for steam purposes. The coals of the State of Washington, and, generally speaking, the coals of the Pacific coast belong to the recent or mezozoic formations, and are destructive to fire-boxes and are not suitable for steam purposes. They are higher in sulphur and ash than those of the true coal era. We find good coals in Colorado, but they cannot be mined cheaply, and the transportation is too expensive for their use upon the seacoast. This proposition applies largely to the western coals, and, consequently, the Vancouver, Australian, and Welsh coals control the market. The coals of Texas and New Mexico are largely unknown, and it is not probable that they will ever compete upon the coast. Therefore, the only practical competitor of the English coals are the coals from the Appalachian coal-field, and the only channel through which these coals can compete with the British coals is through the Inter-oceanic canal. The Appalachian coal-field of the United States embraces nearly 100,000 square miles, and represents the true geological period, and these coals are purer and better than the English coals and far better than the coals of the West, which last are the mezozoic or latter coals. The carboniferous formation in this field (the Appalachian) is an aggregate deposit of more than 9,000 feet, of which there are more than 100 separate, distinct coal veins. These coals lie principally in the Mississippi valley, counting western Pennsylvania in that territory. The annual increase in the consumption since 1880 has been about seven per cent., and the total production for 1894, of England and the United States, was about 343,000,000 tons. This increase will largely come from the Appalachian coal-field, and with transportation facilities no other country can compete therewith. In this field they are to-day mining the cheapest coals in the world. In the State of West Virginia, which is a fair centre of this great field, coal is being mined more cheaply than in Japan. The Japanese pay six cents a day for labor, yet her coal costs $1.56 F. O. B. at the mines. The New South Wales coals and the English coals are always worth $2.25 and $1.75, respectively, per ton at pit mouth, while in the State of West Virginia coal is being mined and loaded at sixty cents per ton on cars at mine and $1.80 F. O. B. at Atlantic tidewater. In other words, the Appalachian coal field in the Mississippi valley can mine and transport coal 400 miles by rail at much less than the cost of the English coal at the pit mouth. Let us take Pittsburgh and West Virginia as a fair test of what benefits this canal will bring to this great article of commerce in this valley. The distance from the Ohio river to New Orleans is 2,000 miles. The cost of transportation to New Orleans is eighty cents from Pittsburgh and sixty-five cents per ton from the mouth of the Kanawha river, in West Virginia. This is cheap transportation. The price of coal of New South Wales, at New Castle, is, as I have said before, $2.25 at the pit mouth. Now transportation by sea will not be as expensive as by river. Transportation by railroad is about one-half per cent. per ton, by steam vessels one-fifth and by sailing vessels one-tenth. Let us quote the price of coal of the markets which we will dominate when we turn our eyes southward and to the Pacific Ocean. The cost of transportation for 15,000 miles from New Orleans to San Francisco is too great for present successful competition. By the Nicaragua canal the distance is reduced by 11,000 miles to a total of 4,000 miles. We will have the advantage of the Welsh coals by nearly 3,000 miles. We can put the Appalachian coals into the San Francisco market at less than market price for the Colorado coals.

In San Francisco the coals at wholesale are about as follows:

Seattle coal,	$6 00
Cardiff coal,	7 25
Australian coal,	6 25
Cumberland coal,	13 00
Lehigh coal,	17 00

As a fair average, West Virginia coal in the Appalachian coal-field can be laid down in the harbor of San Francisco at the rate of from $5.50 to $5.75 per ton. In addition to this there is no comparison between the Seattle coal and the Appalachian coal. The last has the advantage in quality of from $1.50 to $2.25 per ton.

To Mananham, Brazil, the distance from New Orleans is about 3,800 miles; from Newport News, 3,108 miles. I use Newport News as illustrative of the Middle Atlantic ports, such as Norfolk and Baltimore. At this point they use Cardiff coal at $12 per ton. West Virginia coal can be laid down at that harbor at less than $5 per ton. At Pernambuco British and German coal is used. This costs $11 to $15 per ton. From New Orleans to Pernambuco it is 4,580 miles; from Newport News it is 3,888. We can sell them West Virginia coal at that point at $5.50 per ton. At Montevideo, Uruguay, they use British coal, which costs $13 per ton. West Virginia coal can be put in that market at $8 per ton. At Buenos

Ayres they use Cardiff coal, which costs $14. Buenos Ayres is 7,274 miles from New Orleans and 6,582 miles Newport News. West Virginia coal can be placed in this market for $6 per ton. At Acapulco, Mexico, Cardiff and Australian coals are used, which cost $20 per ton. This port is only 2,285 miles from New Orleans and 2,756 miles from Newport News. The Appalachian coal can be placed in that port for less than $5 per ton. At Callao, Peru, Cardiff coal is used, which costs $15 per ton. Callao is 2,984 miles from New Orleans and 3,455 miles from Newport News. West Virginia coal can be placed at that market at $5 to $6 per ton. Valparaiso, Chili, uses Australian coal and Cardiff coal. These coals cost in that port $8 per ton. This port is only 4,254 miles from New Orleans and about 4,725 miles from Newport News, and is almost in a straight line from New Orleans through the canal. West Virginia coal can be placed in that market at $5.60 to $6 per ton.

A fair illustration of what can be accomplished by the Appalachian coal in the South American and West Indian markets was shown in March last, when the Navy Department saved $50,000 by shipping West Virginia coal from the Davis and Elkins mines to our war-ships at Trinidad. Coal averages there $7.30 per ton, but we were able to place the coal on the war-ships at $3.85 per ton. On the other side of the isthmus last year our war-ships were charged $11 a ton for coal, and this year $10.75. Coal could be delivered through the canal for less than $5 a ton.

I have taken both coasts for the reason that as yet little attention has been paid to the Western coast, because little attention has been paid to the trade of South America, and as soon as attention is directed to this trade by reason of the building of the canal, both coasts will be embraced within the limits of American enterprise and industry in this great traffic. The fact that the Appalachian chain contains the greatest number of measures of the best and cheapest coal is beyond discussion. And instead of States like West Virginia, which has within its boundaries 17,000 square miles of coal lying right on the Ohio river, easily accessible to the Gulf of Mexico, mining ten million of tons a year, when this great South American and Pacific trade is opened up, the increase will be incalculable. This will apply to the whole of the Appalachian coal field. With the canal opened the coal trade of the world will be virtually revolutionized.

Let us now consider the article of cotton, the other great staple of commerce in the Mississippi valley. From 1884, the growth of cotton has increased from about six million to upwards of nine million bales in 1892. In eighteen years cotton has brought into the South over five billion two hundred million dollars, and since 1885 our exports of this staple have been three billion eight hundred million dollars. However wonderful these figures may seem in the way of production, and however great has been its influence on mankind at large, all this cotton could have been raised in the State of Texas, and instead of supplying comparatively a limited market, the whole world, if transportation facilities were at hand, could have been supplied with the manufactured article from the United States. Our cotton is largely manufactured by England, and out of ninety-two million spindles, England has forty-five million and our country only fifteen million ; and by reason of England's facilities for transportation this is shipped all over the world and the Mississippi Valley receives nothing but the mere price of the raw article. The 14,000,000 acres of cotton land should have its product sent directly to its destination, and should as surely receive in return the wools, dyes, coffee, and the varied products of the South and the East. With the Nicaraguan canal opened, Japan would be furnished with all her cotton. This cotton should go directly from us. Japan is now beginning to be one of the great cotton manufacturing nations of the earth, and in every line of manufacturing she will soon dominate the East. Look at her momentus progress in this one manufacture. She bought less than one hundred thousand pounds of cotton in 1888; in 1891 she bought seven million pounds of cotton. At this rate it will require but a short time before she will require one-third of the whole cotton crop. She has more than a million spindles, and she has forty millions of people who wear cotton clothing. The ships passing through from New Orleans and across the Pacific Ocean will have a great advantage over those

RAILROAD THROUGH SWAMP BACK OF GREYTOWN.

passing through the Mediterranean Sea and the Suez canal on their way to Japan. The cotton which is used in Japan is principally the long staple cotton, and our cotton is the cotton which is demanded by this trade.

From the South direct should go all the cotton to Japan and China, and the nations of the East. By the opening of the canal this great valley will be brought 1,900 miles nearer Japan, and 2,000 miles nearer the northern coast of China than any of the English markets will be. We will be 1,000 miles nearer Australia than England. With all of this great power of production and manufacture, by reason of the little interest which we have taken in the Eastern and Southern trade, our commerce in cotton has been infinitesimal as compared with England.

In 1890 China imported 61,000,000 of cotton goods, and only 5,000,000 from us. In 1894 we only sold China $2,844,220 in cotton goods; the rest came from England, and this cotton was raised in the valley of the Mississippi With her new awakening, this is rapidly changing. China's rate of progress is only second to that of Japan, and within ten years she will require one-half of our cotton crop. This will revolutionize the trade of the world in cotton. The opening of the canal will make us 1,000 miles nearer Northern China than is Liverpool to-day. That means the ability to undersell. The canal will bring us in closer touch with 500,000,000 of people, who, if they

only use half a pound of cotton each, will use 250,-
000,000 pounds.

This is not an idle dream; there is no conquerer
so swift as cotton. Our country must turn its eyes
to the trade of the East and South. With the canal
in operation every pound of manufactured cotton,
and every yard of cotton fabric can be sold by us to
Western South America. With the canal in operation there will be no longer witnessed the spectacle of
this great republic having not quite $200,000,000 of
interest in the imports and $60,000,000 in the foreign
exports of our Southern neighbors, which together
aggregated last year $1,000,000,000. We only sold
last year to the great republic of Bolivia, $1,233 in
manufactured cotton. We only exported last year
to the republic of Brazil $1,538,680 of cotton and the
manufactures of cotton. We sold to Chili only $462,-
756 in cotton; to Columbia, $200,000; Ecuador, $51,-
992; Peru, $49,999; Venezuela, $543,938 in cotton.
We should control these cotton markets; we are
right near them. We must manufacture the cotton
in sight of the fields in which it is grown. I have
spoken indifferently of the western and the eastern
coasts of South America, because the canal will affect
both coasts by reason of American manufacturers
turning their general attention to this great and
general market. The states embraced in the Ohio
and Mississippi valleys are the states which have
within their bounds one-half of the population of
this great nation; they are states which raise sixty

per cent. of farm products, and own fifty per cent. of the farming land, and sixty per cent. of the live stock of the nation, and one-half of the farming implements.

The ability of this great section to cheaply manufacture, and to largely dominate the trade of the East is shown by the statistics of the manufactures of the Ohio valley. In 1880 the number of manufacturing industries was 89,707, whilst in 1890 it had increased to 115,680. The value of manufactured products in 1890 amounted to $3,346,000,000, about forty per cent. of the total manufactures of this country, as against $1,791,000,000 in 1880, thus showing the enormous increase in ten years of 25,973 manufactories, and $1,555,000,000 in manufactured products. All of this increase was in the face of the fact that in 1893 there went eastward to European nations $83\frac{1}{3}$ per per cent. of our exports, and southward to the American nations nine per cent., northward to British America four per cent., and westward to Pacific nations three and one-half. The workshop has no place in South America. In the Mississippi valley it will have its greatest development.

Another great benefit to the Mississippi valley which will follow from the building of this canal will be that the traffic of the Mississippi river will be largely increased. On this river and its tributaries in 1890 there was a tonnage of 29,405,046. It is almost too great to rightly estimate. The great increase in traffic demanded by the opening up of the nations of the east and of the western coast of South America will intensify the demands for better facilities of traffic upon this river and its tributaries. It will demand the improvement of its channel, and it will demand the improvement of the Ohio, and in addition to this it will most certainly bring about the construction of the canal between Lake Erie and the Ohio river. This is another great dream of commerce which goes hand in hand with the opening of the Central American isthmus.

The only want of manufacturers in the great Ohio valley is the cheap ore of the Lake Superior region. This lake region is part and parcel of the Mississippi valley, and by the building of this last canal will be largely tributary thereto. Out of a total of 11,879,679 tons of production of iron ore for the United States 7,692,548 tons came from the Lake Superior region. From these cheap ores, being brought by the cheap transportation of the Lake canal into the Mississippi valley, will arise thousands of manufactories along these great rivers, which will swell the great volume of commerce passing through the walls of the great Inter-oceanic canal and benefiting the nations of the earth.

The Gulf of Mexico and the Caribbean Sea are more eligibly situated for commerce than any sheets of water upon the globe. The relation of the Mediterranean Sea to Europe does not in any wise compare from a commercial standpoint with the relation of the Gulf of Mexico to the United States. Into this great body of water pour the greatest rivers of the world.

The river basins of Europe, Asia and Africa are but one-fourth in importance as compared with those which empty into the Gulf of Mexico. The Mediterranean Sea is of great length and has an indented coast line, whereas the Gulf of Mexico is compact, and only requires a short time to travel from one of its extremities to the other. It requires a sailing vessel a month to go from the Black Sea into the ocean.

Then in the scope and variety of climate and territory it does not compare with the Gulf of Mexico. The Gulf of Mexico was designed by the hand of nature to hold within its bosom the great commerce of the world. It is within 2,000 miles of the mouth of the Hudson, the Orinoco, the Mississippi, and the Amazon. The mouth of the Amazon and Orinoco, by reason of the trade-winds and the currents are in this ocean, just as the laws of nature have placed the mouth of the Mississippi within the same basin. The currents of the ocean flow into the Gulf of Mexico just as certainly as the currents of the Mississippi and Ohio and Missouri flow within the same limits. The river basins of other countries do not at all compare with the river basins which virtually flow into the Gulf of Mexico. The Mississippi and Missouri rivers, taking their head amidst the great wheat fields of the North, flowing down to the more temperate regions of Missouri, Iowa, Illinois, and Indiana, where the fruits and products of the temperate regions are at their best, continue on to where cotton and the fruits of the South have their highest development. In one and the same period of the year on this magnificent river one sees seed-time and harvest. So it is with the Amazon, which flows through the Andes to the coast, with an extent of products and variety of climate which is not equalled by any other river in the world, excepting the Mississippi, having all of the real advantages of flowing north and south as well as east and west. These two rivers, one having all of the temperatures of the earth, the other having perpetual summer within its limits, both flow into the great American Sea and carry their products there, to be thence distributed to the nations of the earth.

Nature designed here a reciprocal commerce. Each needs that which abounds with the other, and either one can supply every want which the other may feel. The mighty waters of these two great rivers are bound together by the waves of these two seas. These are American seas, and it is an essential of commerce that these waters should be commercially dominated by the American nation. Our cotton and iron and steel and the thousand manufacturers of our great valley are essential to the South American civilization, and the dyes and the rare woods, the rich spices, the indigo, quinine, drugs, wool, hides, india-rubber, the fruit and sugar, and tobacco, coffee, and cocoa, and the thousand other productions of the rich alluvial lands of this great South American valley are imperatively demanded by our civilization.

Every reason of commerce demands that the products of these great rivers shall be commingled in these two great seas and that the isthmus shall no longer separate them from the great marts of the world. This canal will intensify the American feeling, and more than any other work, strengthen and invigorate this great commerce.

When considering what the possibilities of this grand valley would be, when it is filled with a happy, thrifty population, with railroads binding its uttermost boundaries together, with splendid steamers on the breast of its broad waters; with its fertile fields in full bloom of intelligent civilization; with its mines open and its manufactories smoking, Mr. Calhoun well said in his report—" Looking to a not far distant future when this great valley, containing within its limits 1,200,000 square miles, lying in its whole extent in the temperate zone and occupying a position midway between the Atlantic and Pacific Oceans, unequalled in fertility and the diversity of its products, intersected in every direction by the mighty streams, including its tributaries by which it is drained and which supply a continuous navigation of upwards of 10,000 miles, with a coast including both banks of twice that length, shall be crowded with population and its resources fully developed, imagination is taxed in the attempt to realize the magnitude of its commerce."

Another great writer has beautifully said, "Nature has created nothing upon our continent more stupendous than these waters, and they are as much characteristic of the great American Republic, as the institutions, policy, the liberty which distinguish it from all the nations of the earth."

Having thus in a somewhat hurried manner considered the Mississippi valley, let us see how the canal will affect the Pacific coast.

The States of Washington, Oregon, and California in 1880 had 1,114,578 people. In 1894 they had 2,095,598 people. No country has developed as has this section. Senator Dolph shows that the foreign commerce of San Francisco has grown to be as large as the foreign commerce of the United States between 1820 and 1830. The great disadvantage under which the Pacific coast labors is that it is about as great a distance from the Pacific ports, San Francisco, for instance, to Liverpool, as it is to New York. It is only 170 miles further from San Francisco to Liverpool than from San Francisco to New York, whilst from San Francisco to New Orleans it is 212 miles further than from San Francisco to Liverpool. New York, however, by the canal would be 820 miles nearer the Pacific Ocean than by the Union Pacific railroad. The mind can scarcely calculate the great importance of this canal to the Pacific coast. It is almost impossible for the Eastern citizen to appreciate the empire which we have upon the Pacific coast, an empire not alone of territory, but an empire of trade, which should be bound to us by every tie of commerce. The Pacific coast has within its boundary that which we of the middle West and of the East must absolutely have as cheaply as possible. The timber of the East is being rapidly exhausted and will not long stand the great strain which has been put upon the supply. Upon the Pacific coast there are twenty-five millions of acres of the finest timber on the earth, and this timber must be brought by the cheapest route to the great manufacturing centers of our Republic. From the *Lumberman* we got an idea of the great wealth of the section in the matter of timber. Here we have sufficient lumber to supply the world for many decades to come, and no one can form any conception by mere figures.

To compare it with the world's needs of to-day, the truth of this assertion is manifest. Imagine a belt of timber, and by timber we mean a dense forest, almost impenetrable with underbrush and windfalls several feet thick, with hundreds of trees to the acre, many of which are from two to four hundred feet high, so high in fact and so thick that the sun never penetrates the forest of absolute eternal shade; every acre of it contains thousands of feet of the finest kind of timber, every tree waiting for the woodman's ax and the sawman's saw, to be converted into lumber. Imagine such a forest one single mile in width and long enough to girdle the earth three times around its entire circumference, and an additional lap from Puget Sound to the Atlantic Seaboard. It is difficult to grasp such stupendous figures, yet if one can fix such a picture in his imagination he can form some idea of our timber supply; or imagine every city and street and every country road in the United States planked fifty feet in width with lumber from forests in these States and enough left to supply all the demand for building purposes for years to come. As an illustration of the greatness of the traffic, the mills of Washington put out last year 1,800,000,000 shingles. These shingles are being shipped to every part of the United States, they come heavily ladened by the long haul. There is shipped from Puget Sound and the Western coast of the United States an enormous amount of lumber needed for spars and for the various fine manufacturing purposes of this section. This lumber comes burdened to the East by voyage of from fifty days by steamer or one hundred to one hundred and thirty days by sail around Cape Horn, when by the completing of the canal from the time it leaves San Francisco or Portland until it arrives at New York city would be only forty or fifty days by sail and twenty days by steamer, with the distance lessened ten thousand miles.

During the year 1893 the amount of lumber shipped from Puget Sound to foreign ports was 86,428,339 feet. Of this, 11,105,260 went to Great

Britain and the continent of Europe. Every ton of this lumber costs from ten to twelve dollars by the Horn by sail, and from twenty to twenty-five dollars by steam. By rail the rate is too great for successful transcontinental shipment. By the canal the freight will be reduced to eight dollars per thousand, and the time to one-third. The change that will be brought about in this traffic between our Pacific coast and our Atlantic cities will be further appreciated when you understand that from New York to San Francisco, round the Horn, it is 14,840 miles, but by the canal it is but 4,760 miles, showing a saving of 10,080 on the trip out, and 20,160 miles, or almost the circumference of the globe, on the round trip. The present capacity of mills on Puget Sound alone is 1,000,000,000 feet per annum.

There is stumpage to the amount of 400,000,000 of feet on the Pacific coast alone. Consider the effect of the lessening of the freight on this lumber from three to four dollars on the 1,000, and what an impulse it will give to this great industry. Instead of the present comparatively small production of lumber on the Pacific coast, a short time would witness an enormous increase in this industry. A magnificent commerce will be inaugurated which can scarcely be appreciated by the East.

When this route is shortened there will be a saving in one year upon the article of timber alone, of enough to more than construct the canal. Timber is not the only great article of commerce. The immense product of the wheat fields of the Pacific must be considered. Senator Squire estimates that the State of Washington alone has the productive capacity of 200,000,000 bushels of wheat per annum. There was exported last year from Puget Sound, San Francisco and Willamette, Oregon, about 20,000,000 bushels of wheat, and only about 150,000 bushels of this wheat went to countries not tributary to this canal; the rest went to New York and Europe. The canal will reduce freight charges two dollars per ton. From these same ports last year there were shipped nearly 1,300,000 barrels of flour. Of this flour the larger proportion went to countries not tributary to the canal, but still a large proportion of this product will seek the markets of Europe through the canal. The wheat shipped to Liverpool takes about four months, and costs about twenty-six cents per bushel. The cost of transportation around the Horn is not the chief trouble, it is the length of time required by the voyage. When the route to Europe will be lessened nearly 10,000 miles, tremendous will be the increase in this great article of commerce.

It means more than this. By the passage around the Horn wheat is subject to a great change in temperature; by the quicker passage through the canal this great danger will be avoided, and the wheat can be delivered in London in as good a condition as when shipped from San Francisco.

The great wheat-growing competition existing between this country and the Argentine Confederation will within a short time have a very great effect upon the United States. Out of the great abundance of wheat raised on the Pacific coast millions of bushels go to Europe. The Argentine Confederation will be our great competitor. It costs very much more to raise wheat in this country than it does in the Argentine Confederation. If we do not have some great advantage in the way of transportation the cheap production of the Argentine wheat will destroy our European market, for the market is not growing with the production. The building of this canal will place Pacific coast wheat on a very great plane of advantage over the Argentine wheat. To appreciate this statement you must remember that Argentina has her surface only scratched in a few places; yet last year, whilst the United States exported 159,500,000 bushels of wheat, Argentina exported 45,375,000 bushels. Mark you, Argentina is only scratched.

By the canal the time between San Francisco and Liverpool will be reduced to twenty-five days' steam. In addition to the great products of wheat and lumber, there is the fruit trade, and the fur trade, and the fisheries of the Pacific coast, all of which are the largest and best in the world.

Considering the estimate which has been made of the Pacific coast traffic by the promoters of the canal, we find that even their greatest expectations have been distanced by the year 1894. In the articles of green fruits and dried fruit, raisins, and canned goods, the estimate is much greater than was calculated. Senator White states that the State of California produced in these four articles last year 212,000 tons of freight at a valuation of $4,240,000. The same authority estimates that there was over 800,000 gallons of brandy shipped in 1894, and he estimates that no less than two millions of dollars per year will be saved the fruit-growers alone by the construction of the canal. He estimates that on wheat there will always be a saving of two dollars per ton.

In addition to all these actual advantages in shortening the time between the Pacific coast and the East, there will be the greater question of certainty. Around Cape Horn has been since commerce began one of the hardest trips known to the mariner. The great winds around the Cape for the sailing vessels, and the tortuous uncertainty and dangerous passageway through the Straits of Magellan, has been one of the greatest troubles in commerce. When wheat is shipped no one knows when it will reach its destination, or what changes there will be in the market between shipment and arrival, or when the return cargo will be shipped. With the canal there will be a simple run down the coast, a passage through the quiet waters of the canal, and a run up the coast on the eastern side or across the Atlantic Ocean to Europe. More than all of this, it will be an advantage to the Pacific coast by the lessening of railroad freights. The railway freights along the inter-continental railway routes are just simply what the railroad authorities choose to make them. No country

DREDGES WORKING IN CANAL—LOOKING WESTWARD

except the Pacific coast would have grown under such detrimental forces. With the canal completed the Pacific coast will no longer be hampered in the race for commercial supremacy. The previous discussion will do away with the necessity for discussing the effect of the canal upon the eastern part of this country. Let us turn from the commercial to the diplomatic and military view of the canal.

The diplomatic side of this question is very interesting. What right has this government to build or to assist in building this canal? What rights have this government under the existing treaties between the countries of the world? What interest can she take in it? We answer, that leaving out the countries of Nicaragua and Costa Rica, this country has the paramount interest in this work. We grant that no commercial nation should be discriminated against in the matter of the passage of its commerce through the canal, and whilst this is willingly conceded, still we contend that our government should never, under any circumstances, allow any other than itself to be the dominating power in this great enterprise. Every patriotic citizen of the United States believes that our country should be the controlling influence in matters pertaining to the construction and operation of this canal. All of us concur in the proposition that this government should be the dominating power in this hemisphere. British statesmen, fifty years ago, clearly saw that there would be but one power which could in any wise contend with England for commercial supremacy. The spirit of rivalry is not even of such late growth. It has been seen and understood by British statesmen for 200 years. In the minister's remonstrance to parliament in 1670, speaking of our sailors, they clearly stated that which expressed then, as it does now, English sentiment.

"They violate our ordinances of trade with impunity, and our navigation laws, the last of which with infinite pains we have devised, they trample under foot with disdain. Their traders sally out upon the deep; we find them seeking entrance in all ports of Europe; they even encourage foreigners to trade with them."

With the wise commercial foresight which has always characterized British statesmen, they saw that they must control every avenue of commerce. As a matter of fact but few remained free from British aggression and British control. Understanding the far-reaching importance of this canal and knowing that every commercial reason demanded that the United States should control it when built, the British government stepped in and undertook to have a joint control with the United States. It sought to accomplish this by putting forward claim to part of the territory through which the canal would pass; England did not take the Mosquito coast absolutely as her possession, but seizing a part of Nicaragua territory upon a mere claim, she crowned a king from Nicaraguan subjects and virtually established a protectorate over the territory. This course was taken by England to avoid the question as to her infraction of the Monroe doctrine, and was in-intended solely to force upon the United States a joint control of the canal. In 1850 the two governments made what is known as the Clayton-Bulwer convention, the first clause in which treaty provided that "the governments of the United States and Great Britain hereby declare that neither one or the other will ever obtain or maintain for itself any exclusive control over the said ship canal." This clause is the real gist of the whole treaty on the part of England, and is the condition for which she had been really contending. The convention further provided that "neither one government or the other will ever colonize or assume, or exercise any dominion over Nicaragua, Costa Rica or the Mosquito coast, or any part of Central America." In other words, it provided that neither government should exercise exclusive control over the canal. The whole treaty shows that it was intended that neither one or the other of the parties to the convention should exclude the other from the benefits arising from the great work. How does this treaty stand to-day? In the opinion of great international lawyers it is void for the reason that the canal was not completed as was then contemplated, and from the further reason that the terms of the treaty were not complied with on the part of Great Britain. Furthermore, any provision as a matter of politics or

State policy which will allow the government of Great Britain to participate in the supreme control of this canal would not to-day be tolerated by the American people. This is a plain way of putting it, but it is a very honest declaration of the sentiment of the whole nation. At that time, public sentiment did not stand where it does to-day, and the conditions under which the treaty was consummated are not the conditions of to-day.

Irrespective of any question of the change of public sentiment and the change of the condition of affairs, the treaty has been abrogated by the acts of Great Britain herself. She systematically, and, in the face of the treaty, colonized the Balize settlement, which has been increased territorially, and from a governmental standpoint, until to-day it is a part of the imperial government. The Mosquito coast also was virtually made into a dependency of the British.

This policy was carried out by Great Britain right in the face of the Clayton-Bulwer treaty, which some people are in the habit of resurrecting in order to do away with the construction of the canal by the United States. When this treaty was considered the Suez canal was not constructed, and in the control of Great Britain, and the whole burden of the proceedings show that the immediate completion of the canal was contemplated. This was in 1850. Such being the status of affairs, in 1867, seventeen years after the Clayton-Bulwer treaty, the government of the

United States concluded with the Republic of Nicaragua a fair, liberal treaty. Article 14 of said treaty is as follows: "The Republic of Nicaragua hereby grants to the United States and their citizens and property the right of transit between the Atlantic and Pacific Oceans through the territory of that republic on any route of communication, natural or artificial, whether by land or by water, which may now or hereafter exist or be constructed under the authority of Nicaragua, to be used in the same manner and upon equal terms by both republics and their respective citizens—the Republic of Nicaragua, however, reserving its rights of soverignty over the same." The United States further guaranteed the neutrality and innocent use of the canal, and this government also has the right to carry munitions of war to either of the free ports established by the Nicaraguan government, and the treaty provided further that should it become necessary to supply military force it will provide the requisite force, but that the government of the United States may do so upon failure on the part of the Nicaraguan government. This treaty further provides the right of Congress of the United States to legislate so as to provide the laws for the carrying into effect this treaty. The treaty is a very broad one. The British government two years afterwards made a similar treaty to this one with the Nicaraguan government. This treaty is subject to the provisions of our treaty. In 1884 Mr. Frelinghuysen negotiated a very broad treaty with Nicaragua. This treaty virtually granted sovereignty within the limits of Nicaragua to the United States, and was withdrawn by the President from consideration by the Senate.

In 1887 Nicaragua made a concession to Mr. A. G. Manacal for an American company for the building and operating of the canal for ninety-nine years. Very large and important provisions were conceded to this company, which was composed exclusively of American citizens, but all of these concessions are under, and entirely consistent with, the treaty of 1867, which gives the largest latitude on the part of the American government in the operation and defence of this canal. The bill embodying these provisions and concessions was the one which was introduced into Congress, and was the one which was elaborately discussed in the last Congress. Since the Clayton-Bulwer treaty public sentiment has entirely changed, and the conditions have entirely changed. This is the only trade avenue not now in the control of the British government, and this is of more vital importance to the United States than any other enterprise, commercial or otherwise, since the formation of this government. It is virtually a continuation of the coast line of the United States. In connects and binds together our great republic, and every consideration of diplomacy and self-interest makes our citizens say distinctly but firmly that, notwithstanding any question of legal casuistry as to treaty obligations with England, the government of the United States, in the management and control of this great avenue of commerce, will permit no interference from other nations. Its innocent neutrality, so far as commerce is concerned, will be guaranteed by our nation. No larger tolls will be charged the citizens of any other government than is charged the citizens of our republic. No greater burden will be put upon any other nation's commerce than will be put upon our own; but when questions arise concerning the control and management of this canal, in moments of supreme interest to our government, it must be distinctly understood by the nations of the earth that we will be supreme. No other nation but England will gainsay this plain, sensible and palpable proposition, and it does not lie in the mouth of a government which, in the face of neutrality treaties, for three days closed the Suez canal in order to assert its eminence and control therein, to say that in a trade avenue of such vital importance to our government that we shall not absolutely control. Anyhow, what do neutrality treaties mean? They mean simply that the power which has the biggest guns and the fastest ships and the closest position to the neutral zone will seize it. That is the history of neutral zones at the moment of a contest with arms. Then why give up our manifest right to be in the controlling position in case of trouble?

President Hayes well states our proposition: "The policy of this government is a canal under American control. The United States cannot consent to the surrender of this control to any European government. If existing treaties between the United States and other nations, or if the rights of sovereignty or property by other nations stand in the way of this policy, a contingency which is not apprehended, suitable steps should be taken by just and liberal connections to promote and establish the American policy on this subject consistently with the rights of the nations to be affected by it. The capital invested by corporations and citizens of other countries in such an enterprise must, in a great measure, look for protection to one or more of the great powers of the world. No European power would intervene for such protection without measures on this condition which the United States would deem wholly inadmissible. If the protection of the United States is relied upon, the United States must exercise such control as will enable this country to protect its national interest and maintain the rights of those who provide capital to embark in the work. . . . . .

Our commercial interest in it is greater than that of all other countries, while its relation to our power and our prosperity as a nation, to our means of defence, our unity, peace and safety are matters of paramount concern to the people of the United States. No other great power would, under similar circumstances, fail to assert a rightful control over a work so closely and vitally affecting its interests and welfare."

In the opinion of some people the Clayton-Bulwer treaty is alive. Surely the question of its life and death can, at the utmost, be but a question of doubt. In whose favor shall we solve the doubt? In favor of England? Doubt and vacillation have already given her Egypt and the Suez canal. Our plain duty is to give our country the benefit of the doubt, and say firmly and plainly that no trammels except our treaty obligations to Nicaragua would in anywise interfere with our decision. This is the manner in which England decides all questions of doubt in which she may be interested. Shall we be less fair with ourselves? Shall we for mere sentiment give up our plain right and for want of patriotism throw away a kingdom of commerce? If we do so, what we now throw away in diplomacy, sooner or later, we will be compelled to fight for in war. The diplomatic discussion brings to us the kindred and incidental question of the purely strategical and military importance of the work. Every interest of the United States demands that the Gulf of Mexico and the Caribbean Sea should, from a military standpoint, be really American seas, absolutely under the military strategical domain of the United States. To carry out the Monroe doctrine it is necessary that our government have power right at hand to easily handle. This government must protect its southern neighbors from the actual control and occupancy of trans-continental and non-republican powers. This debt, by her power, location and importance, is forced upon this country.

I do not mean by this proposition to assert mere jingoism. I do not believe that this government should be ready to take up every quarrel which a South American country may have with the European powers. The Monroe doctrine does not mean that this country should act the bully in South American complications with European governments. The Monroe doctrine does mean, however, the vigorous determination on the part of this country that there shall be no permanent aggression upon South American States by European governments. It means that we will not allow the form of free American governments which we have recognized to be changed by the influence of Continental governments. It means that no combination of European governments against American governments will be tolerated on the part of this government. And it means more than that—that we will not allow the permanent widening and extending of European colonization and influence within the territorial limits of South America. It expressly says that with "the existing colonies or dependencies of any European power we have not interfered and shall not interfere; but with the governments which have declared their independence, which we have on great consideration and just principles recognized, we could not view any interposition for the purpose of oppressing them or controlling in any other manner their destiny by European powers in any other light than as a manifestation of an unfriendly disposition towards the United States."

I take it that the Monroe doctrine means something. That President Monroe when he said—"We owe it, therefore, to candor and to the amicable relations existing between the **United** States and those powers to declare **that we should** consider any attempt on their part to extend their systems to any portion of this hemisphere as dangerous to our peace and safety. . . . . .
We could not view any interposition for the purpose of oppressing or controlling in any other manner their destiny by any European power in any other light than as a manifestation of an unfriendly disposition towards the United States"—meant that the European governments could not reconquer and recolonize and divide South American States. The Allied European governments at the time of the enunciation of this doctrine so understood that he meant exactly what he said at that time and took their hands away from the South American territory. If the Monroe doctrine did not mean just what it said, or, if to-day, it has changed its meaning, then eliminate it from our unwritten law, for it is but sounding brass and tinkling cymbals.

Despite the refining influence induced by ultraconservative political considerations the common people of the United States believe that the doctrine is to-day just what it was when it destroyed the alliance of European sovereigns who attempted to partition the territory of South America among them.

I confess that from a political standpoint I cannot differentiate between England dismembering Venezuela, a free republican government, and the Allied sovereigns partitioning South America among themselves. Therefore, if the Monroe doctrine is to be maintained this country must be potent from a naval or strategical view in the Southern seas.

The Gulf of Mexico will, from its location, become the centre of the largest carrying trade of the world. The greater part of it will be American. Its position is such that it dominates the richest territory in the world, the heart and centre of the United States, the great valley of the Mississippi. Its defence is not local as would be the defence of the harbor of a great city. Its loss would affect Maine as well as Mississippi. Every ship owner or cargo owner having an interest in the great carrying trade of the West would be affected.

Says a distinguished statesman, once at the head of the war department, "And it must be borne in mind that the evils which would result from the temporary occupancy of the delta of the Mississippi or from a successful blockade of the coasts of the Gulf of Mexico would not only injure the prosperity of these States, but would deeply affect the interest of the whole Union. No reasonable expense, therefore, ought to be spared to guard against such a casualty."

The canal will be the virtual southern boundary

of the United States, and from a military standpoint it would be ruinous to the United States for any other country to control it.

Could any Central American state control it? The first revolution would put it in the hands of some strong European power, and any European power in this hemisphere would be inimical to the interests of this government. No private party or corporation could hold it. No weak power can hold it. It must be in a masterful grasp. In case of war, and war must be considered, the strategical relations of this canal to this hemisphere will be very much more important than the relation of the Suez to the Eastern hemisphere. Consider its strategical situation and the great military possibilities it develops. Careful surveys of every portion of Central America have shown that the only feasible route between the oceans is the Nicaraguan route, and that route is through the great fresh water lake of Nicaragua. This lake has sufficient capacity to hold the navies of the world, and it is the only portion of Central America where health reigns. It is in the gap of the mountains through which the cool trade winds blow and prevent fever and miasma. Here is the only place in Central America where the stricken or wounded sailor can enjoy the coolness of a mountain sanitarium, with fresh water and tropical fruits in abundance. At Panama men died like flies and were as little considered. At Nicaragua, out of 1,600 men employed by the Nicaraguan company for four months, only two died, and from 200 men from a colder climate, not one died of disease incident to the climate. It is a lake whose soft water will cleanse the bottom of the ship from every impurity, and where our country may place its dry docks, hospitals, coal stations, warehouses, repair shops, and arrange all the paraphernalia necessary for naval affairs. The treaty of 1867 with Nicaragua is broad enough to give us the right to erect fortifications for our soldiers sent there under this treaty. It is broad enough to allow our navy to be stationed there as a base for strategical operations in both oceans. If it is not, the Republic of Nicaragua has shown that its Americanism is sufficiently liberal to confer upon us such powers as are necessary to make us the controlling influence in the canal. We ask no sovereignty over Central American territory. We do not seek to invade the traditions of our past by assuming sovereignty over any other than our own territory, but it would be the husk without the corn to present us the right to supply millions of money to build this great work, and say that we have not the power to protect it by works sufficient for that purpose. For us to refuse to do so would be to evince a spirit of national self-abnegation and weak sentimentalism which would be viewed among the nations with derision and contempt.

With the prescience which seems almost miraculous, England readily discovered that on this continent would rise her great naval rival. With the

RAILROAD BRIDGE ACROSS BENARD CREEK.

energy which has characterized that nation, she steadily set herself to work to reach out and environ this government with commercial outposts in times of peace, and fortifications in times of war. Considering her single idea predominance, we can well say of England—

"Through the ages one increasing purpose runs."

Seeing that the undeveloped territory of South America would be one of the trade emporiums of the world, she has erected her military force so that every merchant vessel sailing from New York or Boston, or any of our eastern ports, on its way to the rich trading fields of South America must pass British fortifications and British naval stations. She has located great fortifications at the Bermudas, within two days of New York. On the Pacific and on the Atlantic and on the Gulf of Mexico she is ready to strike our defenceless cities and interfere with our commerce. In Europe, Asia, and Africa her frowning forts and shotted guns control every vital position, and the black hulls of her men-of-war darken every ocean.

"She has encompassed the whole world with her outposts and military possessions, and her morning drum-beat, following the sun in its course, keeping company with the hours, encircles the globe with one continuous and unbroken peal of the martial airs of England."

Like the stars of the sky, her coaling stations and

naval depots dot the Pacific Ocean. She owns the Bahamas, the Windward and the Leeward islands, Jamaica, Tobago, and Trinidad, and to-day can absolutely bottle up the mouth of the Mississippi. Every pass into the Gulf of Mexico is controlled by her forts. Our vessels on their way to California must pass in times of war through a sea controlled by islands from whose harbors English men-of-war, thoroughly equipped with every paraphernalia of war and every appliance necessary for offence and defence. She has located herself on the continent of South America, where she can strike at our commerce and absolutely drive us out of the country. Above us on the western coast is the great strategical and military post on Vancouver Island, from whence she can swoop down upon our States on the Pacific. From the military and naval depots of Canada she can quickly reach our great eastern ports.

In every part of the New World the government of the United States is menaced by English trading stations in times of peace and by British fortifications in times of war. So it is with the Old World: She sits like a lion crouched at Gibraltar; she controls Cyprus and Malta, and Ceylon, and the Suez canal, and Egypt; and despite the power and diplomacy of European nations, the Mediterranean Sea is to-day a British lake. She has drawn around the whole world a wall of forts, from which from one to the other can be heard the boom of her guns.

When I speak of England I mention her in no

spirit of acrimony, but rather with a feeling of admiration for the country which has, in and out of season, so carefully protected her commerce and her military interests.

Our next war will be virtually a naval war. It will consist almost exclusively of naval conflicts between hostile fleets, preying on the enemy's merchant service and the levying of tribute on our defenceless cities. To be effectual in protection or aggression our fleet must be in position to give aid either to the Atlantic or Pacific Oceans, with the power to meet the Pacific squadron at San Francisco in seven days and, if necessary, fight a battle on the coast of Mexico, and within twenty days' time be back in the harbor of the lake, and then within a short sail be able to protect New Orleans or to steam to Kingston, Gaudaloupe, or the Bermudas. If necessary, in five days it could be defending Savannah, then join our fleet at Hampton Roads, or be back at Mobile, and then through the canal to the coast of Peru or Chili. Suppose, for instance, there should be a serious controversy on the coast of Brazil. Consider the disadvantage our government would be compelled to undergo. The Pacific squadron would be compelled to steam down the coast of South America, around Cape Horn to the shoulder of South America, ten thousand miles, when in all probability the trouble would have been over or an irreparable injury have been done to our commercial interests.

There are two passes into the Gulf of Mexico. One

is from the Atlantic Ocean through the straits of Florida, between the island of Cuba and the Florida Keys. The Bahama Islands lie absolutely across this great and chief pass, and every ship from New York or Boston, or the Eastern coast, bound to the mouth of the Mississippi or the Gulf of Mexico must pass through a cordon of British fortified islands. These islands stretch from a short distance of the southeastern Florida coast to within a short distance of Hayti. The other pass is from the Caribbean Sea and is through the channel of Yucatan, between Cuba and Yucatan. This pass is dominated by the magnificent island of Jamaica, in whose land locked harbor of Kingston 1,000 ships may safely lie. Nearer yet to the pass lie the Little and Great Cayman Islands, both British possessions. More than this, unless ships will enter into the Gulf of Mexico through the straits of Florida, passing the Bahama Islands, they will be compelled to go through the Windward Passage, between Cuba and Hayti, or through the Mona Passage, between Hayti and Porto Rico, or through the passage between the Windward Islands into the Caribbean Sea.

In every case commerce will be compelled to pass by the island of Jamaica. The last passage through the Windward Islands, by reason of the tortuous navigation, would be almost impossible, and for the further reason that the British absolutely dominate the entrance into the Caribbean Sea from the shoulder of South America.

In addition to this **great cordon of islands** from the Great Bahama Island, stretching from near the Coast of Florida through the Bahama Islands, and Leeward and Windward Islands to the islands of Trinidad, right on the coast of South America, there are the Central American Provinces of British Honduras and the Mosquito coast, which are parts of the very continent which must be pierced by this canal.

England's strategical and commercial encroachments have not been confined alone to the islands of the Caribbean Sea and of the Gulf of Mexico. Her present contention with Venezuela is fraught with even more vital consequence to this government than any other in which England has ever engaged. The success of her attempt to control the mouth of the Orinoco river with its vast military and commercial importance will virtually turn over Northeastern South America to Great Britain. With the mouth of the Orinoco in the hands of England every interest demands that we have a fleet in the canal or near to Western South America. The importance of this river can scarcely be realized. It dominates the best parts of Venezuela and a large part of Columbia. Venezuela has a territory of 597,960 square miles, and is greater in extent than Texas, Colorado, Idaho, and California. This great river is three miles wide, 600 miles from its mouth, and has tides to the city of Bolivar, nearly 400 miles from the ocean. It has 436 affluents, some of them great rivers. Venezuela is one of the great States of South America, and the Orinoco and Amazon rivers, as I have said before, have their outlet with the Mississippi and in the straits of Florida, and should not be tributary to any other than a South American government. The valley of the Orinoco is one of the richest in the world. The climate of the State is magnificent and is as varied, by reason of its different elevations, as any on the globe. The plains are rich and fertile, and the mountains are filled with rich minerals and clothed with magnificent and rare woods. Here the best cereal and the most luscious fruit grow side by side, and it is a land fitted by nature to be the grazing field of the world.

From the Orinoco by navigable stream you may pass to the Amazon. With the Orinoco in the grasp of England in times of war no American ship, unless protected, can safely pass Northern South America on its way to the mouth of the Amazon. Within England's control will be a splendid harbor, backed by a rich country, flowing with milk and honey, and reaching almost to the other ocean.

In every instance, every strategical point along the northern coast of South America, along Central America and the Gulf of Mexico, is controlled by British possessions and British fortifications, and the only possibility of this government protecting the vast interests of the Mississippi valley and of its South American commerce and of its southern carrying trade in general would be from the fortifications and the land-locked harbor of the Interoceanic canal.

Can we longer refuse to accept our destiny? Is there not danger that the crown may not again be offered us? Is it wise statesmanship for us to delay this important enterprise? Year by year our increasing commerce will surely demand that we have a strong hand beyond our mere territorial limits.

It is true that the mighty tread of our free people shakes the world; that we have conquered a continent and have hewn the path of a splendid civilization broad and plain from sea to sea; that we have conquered in all our wars with alien foes, and the government has remained steady and vigorous amidst internecine strife. Yet in the day of our power, let us look ahead, and not wantonly throw away the broad empire of a world's commerce. Let us remember that our republican form of government is only a trial, and that ere long we may be compelled alone to face the combined jealousies of the Old World. Whilst we can, let us seize the gateway of the world's commerce, and with these gates in our strong hands we can laugh to scorn the combined jealousies of the monarchies of the Old World.

A great writer has said that the twentieth century will witness two colossal nations to which other nations of the earth will be as pigmies—the United States of America and Russia. The despotic government of Russia may delay her ultimate destiny, but with commerce untrammeled and barriers broken down our country will brook no delay in her majestic career. If we are but true to our traditions, and grasp our opportunities firmly, our people will early see the day when the dusky foot of the Eastern mother will tread the pedals of the American sewing machine; when the merry click of the American reaper will be heard on the banks of the Ganges; when in Eastern lands beautiful structures rivaling the Taj will rear their fair heads, fashioned by the keen edge of American tools; when American engines will rush and roar in the valleys of the Rio Negro, the Amazon and the Orinoco; when the products of American looms will be sold at the foot of the Himalayas and sought for in the valleys of the Andes; and when the seas will be merry with the laugh of the American sailor and bright with the gleam of our sails. Then the genius of our free institutions, permeating and rehabilitating, glorifying the nations of the earth, will have subserved its purpose in making all nations co-heirs with us in the blessings of free government.

With this grand destiny so near consummation, surely our magnificent energy will break away the last barrier to the peoples of the earth, and then—

> "Creation's heir
> The World, the World is mine."

The Monroe Doctrine.

The Monroe Doctrine.

Edmund Burke, the greatest of European statesmen during the eighteenth century, has traced the history of European settlements in the two Americas with a master hand. Robertson's History of America to a large extent is an elaboration of Burke's admirable compendium.

No intelligent American can read this compendium by the great orator and statesman without becoming convinced that the domination of Europe in the affairs of this hemisphere—"cisatlantic affairs," as Jefferson called them—has been the darling dream of thrones since the discovery of America by Columbus. For a century and a half before the American Revolution, England and France waged constant war in North America for supremacy. Thanks to her American colonies and the Indian Confederacy of the Iroquois or Five Nations, England finally vanquished France and snatched the sceptre from the Bourbons on the Heights of Abraham.

Prescott with luminous pen has written the history of Mexico and South America and depicted the conflicts of the Spanish and Portuguese adventurers with the Red men and Incas to plant the colors of Castile and Portugal in that great southern division of America. Everywhere the same story is repeated; man's lust of dominion is written in the blood of the Aborigines who were gradually driven back and exterminated before the inroads of the audacious race of Japhet.

France aided the thirteen revolting American colonies to break the yoke of bondage to England and establish the Independence of the United States. The prediction of Count de Vergennes was fulfilled. In 1759, when that astute French statesman received the news of the death of the illustrious Montcalm and the consequent destruction of the fair fabric of New France on this continent, he attributed to the Anglo-American colonies the chief credit for the result, and declared they were now in a position to help themselves. France was gone, England would soon follow; the latter's triumph would prove a fatal one. "Her colonies will no longer need her protection," said he; "she will call on them to contribute toward supporting the burdens they have helped to bring on her, and they will answer by striking off all dependence."

Thus the rivalry of thrones subserved the cause of liberty, and Louis XVI., no less than Washington, contributed to make the new world its future home. The Titanic wars of Napoleon followed and kept our first four presidents in a sea of troubles while striving to steer the bark of the infant republic clear of those "entangling alliances" which formed the burden of warning in the farewell address of the father of his country. The massive strength and saving common sense of Washington, the prophetic vision and incomparable genius for government of Jefferson, rescued the United States in the days of our infancy from the vortex which made Europe a charnel house of carnage. He who reads the general correspondence and writings of Jefferson will discover that that great lawgiver and founder of government was the first man in America to read the riddle of the future aright, and to mark off the boundaries between republicanism and monarchy in the two Americas.

What the inspired Bishop Berkeley prophesied in his verses on the prospect of planting arts and learning in America, Jefferson's world-embracing vision not only described as the poet dreamed it, but shaped it into legislation and the accomplished facts of statecraft:

> "Westward the course of empire takes its way;
> The four first acts already past,
> A fifth shall close the drama with the day;
> Time's noblest offspring is the last."

Out of the French Revolution a man arose who controlled the whirlwind and rode the storm. The mission of Napoleon Bonaparte seemed to be to plague the Pharaohs of the earth. He turned their rage into the plaything of his ambition, and by his stupendous genius broke them like a horse-tamer into abject submission to his will. All the latent and active power of the French Revolution became the instrument of his aggrandisement, and kings fled aghast before the colossal armaments of the man of destiny. The finger of God finally traced the handwriting on the wall, and Napoleon was weighed in the scales which men could not set, and he was found wanting. Puny monarchs who had cringed to his knees, trembled before his frown and striven among themselves for his favors, now vaunted their prowess as his conquerors, and sat down at the Congress of Vienna to divide the spoils. In the day of their terror these same monarchs confessed their impotency, petitioned heaven for deliverance in sackcloth and ashes, and humbly promised to give to God all the credit for any success over the terrible Emperor of the French. "The Redeemer," exclaimed Alexander of Russia, "inspired every thought comprised in the alliance, all the principles it announces. It is not our work, it is God's." This was the treaty of the Holy Alliance ratified on the 26th of September, 1815. Read in the light of history, the real issue between Napoleon and the Allies was not the vindication of the rights of nations, but which of them should have the coveted power to violate them. The Allies won, and their Holy Alliance became a scandalous conspiracy against the liberties of mankind.

The Monroe doctrine proclaimed in 1823, has been unequivocally reasserted in 1895 by President Cleveland. The British government, whose encroachments upon the territory of Venezuela have been steadily increasing for fifty years past, was invited by this government to submit to arbitration all questions in dispute between England and the South American republic. Lord Salisbury in his reply not only rejected the invitation to arbitrate, but declared the Monroe doctrine to be a dead and buried issue of the past, wholly obsolete at the present day, and never pertinent or applicable except against the Holy Alliance in the early part of the present century, when the peculiar circumstances of the South American republics, which had then recently thrown off the Spanish yoke, rendered the doctrine of some interest and importance to the nations of Europe and America. His lordship asserts for Mr. Canning, Prime Minister of England at that day, chief credit over its putative author, Mr. Monroe, for the idea behind the doctrine.

Mr. Cleveland's message to Congress is the proper reply to this British manifesto. It breaks through the cobwebs of diplomatic garrulity and proclaims America's unalterable purpose to stand by the Monroe doctrine as the unwritten, but not less sacred law than the Constitution itself. That doctrine was expressed by President Monroe in the following memorable words:

1. "The political system of the Allied powers is essentially different in this respect from that of America. This difference proceeds from that which exists in their respective governments. And to the defense of our own, which has been achieved by the loss of so much blood and treasure, and matured by the wisdom of their most enlightened citizens, and under which we have enjoyed unexampled felicity, this whole nation is devoted. We owe it, therefore, to candor

and to the amicable relations existing between the United States and those powers to declare that we should consider any attempt on their part to extend their system to any portion of this hemisphere as dangerous to our peace and safety. With the existing colonies or dependencies of any European power we have not interfered, and shall not interfere. But with the governments who have declared their independence and maintained it, and whose independence we have, on great consideration and on just principle, acknowledged, we could not view any interposition for the purpose of oppressing them, or controlling in any other manner their destiny, by any European power, in any other light than as the manifestation of an unfriendly disposition toward the United States."

2. "Our policy in regard to Europe, which was adopted at an early stage of the wars which have so long agitated that quarter of the globe, nevertheless remains the same, which is not to interfere in the internal concerns of any of its powers; to consider the government *de facto* as the legitimate government for us; to cultivate friendly relations with it, and to preserve those relations by a frank, firm and manly policy; meeting in all instances the just claims of every power, submitting to injuries from none. But, in regard to these continents, circumstances are eminently and conspicuously different. It is impossible that the Allied powers should extend their political system to any portion of either continent without endangering our peace and happiness; nor can any one believe that our Southern brethren, if left to themselves, would adopt it of their own accord. It is equally impossible, therefore, that we should behold such interposition, in any form, with indifference."

An American commission to examine and report upon the true divisional line between Venezuela and British Guiana was recommended to Congress by President Cleveland, and by that body was immediately and unanimously authorized by law. The President has appointed the commissioners and the country awaits their report. That report will furnish a light unto our feet whithersoever or into whatever thorny paths its recommendations may lead.

In this crisis the American people have not been slow to express their sympathy with and approval of the Democratic President and the Republican Congress—happily diverse in politics—to make their unity in patriotic duty more impressive, and their unanimous support of the Monroe doctrine a notice to mankind that behind that vote seventy millions of freemen stand solidly arrayed.

Certain individuals who haunt the stock-markets have expressed dissent. Like the Tories who beset Washington in the Revolution, they are on the English side. Should the tide rise these mercenaries would be swept away in the resistless flood. In the meantime it more concerns us to know we are right in holding fast, as by the horns of the altar, to the great American principle of non-intervention by Europe with the free governments in this hemisphere, which Jefferson taught Monroe to proclaim in the days of our infancy, and which Cleveland now reasserts after we have hardened into the bone and gristle of manhood.

Secretary Olney, in his correspondence on this grave question, has recapitulated the precedents laid down by this government by many of his predecessors in the State Department, all having been in strict line with the principles of the Monroe doctrine. He learnedly reviews the pretensions of British Guiana to Venezuelan territory, and shows by an elaborate statement of the various British surveys and claims that the territory at first only conjecturally assumed to belong to British Guiana, 30,000 square miles, constantly grew in extent as the years went by, and that every new survey became but a stage and resting-place in the accelerated progress, till the claim to 30,000 has grown into one of 109,000 square miles—a territory, which, as a distinguished writer has pointed out, is to-day 40,000 square miles larger than the entire six States of New England.

Senator Lodge has followed on the same side in a speech on the floor of the Senate, in which he has traced the growth of this British claim with great research, no little accuracy, and true American patriotism. He establishes the proposition that the balance of power in Europe is not more important to its governments than the Monroe doctrine is to the two Americas. Mr. John Bach McMaster, the historian, has also contributed several interesting papers to the controversy, in which the origin and history of the Holy Alliance, and the respective messages of President Monroe, in 1823, of President Polk, in 1845 and 1848, and of President Buchanan, in 1860, are all discussed with fullness and ability.

Of these several papers those of Secretary Olney are the least partisan. He does not even criticise Secretary Clayton for neglecting to assert the Monroe doctrine in his negotiations with Lord Bulwer, although the astute Lord Salisbury, in his reply, calls attention to Mr. Clayton's unfortunate *faux pas*. His Lordship says: " It (the Monroe doctrine) is said to have largely influenced the government of that country in the conduct of its foreign affairs; though Mr. Clayton, who was Secretary of State under President Taylor, expressly stated that the administration had in no way adopted it." But neither Senator Lodge nor Mr. McMaster has observed Mr. Olney's forbearance to heap so serious a reproach upon an American statesman as is implied in the gratuitous statement that two of them neglected to plant themselves upon the time-honored doctrine. Senator Lodge goes out of his way to arraign Mr. Calhoun "as the only American statesman of any standing who has tried to limit its scope." The case of Mr. Clayton, mentioned by Lord Salisbury, and once scathingly reviewed in the Senate by the illustrious Stephen A. Douglas, evidently escaped the attention of the senator from Massachusetts.

Mr. McMaster indulges in a similar partisan misrepresentation of the attitude of James K. Polk on the same subject in 1826, as contrasted with his course as President in 1845 and again in 1848. Senator Lodge, with the exuberance of the rhetorician, takes the world into his confidence, and as he gets ready to send a Parthian shaft after Mr. Calhoun, he pauses to inform us that "John Quincy Adams may be considered as the real author of the Monroe doctrine." The subject is too grave for partisan and ill-timed flings. Thus the opponents of the great American doctrine, first enunciated by Mr. Monroe, are fond of quoting the advice of Washington against "entangling alliances," forgetting all the time that the father of his country, if not the author, was the most earnest champion of our first great alliance—that with France in the Revolution. They forget that Jefferson, the constant guide whom the wise Monroe delighted to follow, was the man to whom he submitted the Rush-Canning correspondence on this memorable occasion, and that it was upon Jefferson's advice he acted in writing the message which has linked his name with national glory, and will transmit it to the latest posterity consecrated in the affections of his countrymen forever.

It may not be beneath the dignity of the subject to let Mr. Calhoun answer the charge against him in his own words, wherein it will also appear that the credit attempted to be snatched from Monroe and given to Adams by Senator Lodge, is bestowed by a witness, who was present during these great transactions, on him to whom the whole world accredits it— honest, fearless, plain-spoken James Monroe. It is worthy of observation that Mr. Adams subsequently repudiated this doctrine by his course in opposing the annexation of Texas, over which England and France were then seeking to establish a protectorate.

In his speech in the Senate May 15, 1848, on the proposed occupation of Yucatan, Mr. Calhoun, in speaking of the Monroe doctrine and Mr. Adams's part therein, said : " When the chairman of the Committee on Foreign Relations addressed the Senate a few days since, he related a conversation which he had with Mr. Adams in reference to this declaration; and according to his statement, if I heard him aright, and he be correctly reported, Mr. Adams, in applying his observations to the whole of these declarations, stated that they all originated with himself, and were unknown to the other members of the cabinet until they appeared in Mr. Monroe's message. There certainly must be a mistake on the part of Mr. Adams, or that of the chairman of the Committee on Foreign Relations, as to the two first of these declarations. The history of the transactions, the Senator will perceive, if he examines the documents, shows distinctly that they came through Mr. Rush—originating, not with Mr. Adams, but Mr. Canning—and were first presented in the form of a proposition from England. I recollect as distinctly as I do any event of my life, that all the papers in connection with this subject were submitted to the members before the cabinet met, and were duly considered. Mr. Adams, then, in speaking of the whole as one, must have reference to the declaration relative to colonization. As respects this his memory does not differ much from mine. My impression is, that it never became a subject of deliberation in the cabinet. I so stated when the Oregon question was before the Senate. I stated it in order that Mr. Adams might have an opportunity of denying it, or asserting the real state of the facts. He remained silent, and I presume that my statement is correct—that this declaration was inserted after the cabinet deliberation. It originated entirely with Mr. Adams, without being submitted to the cabinet, and it is, in my opinion, owing to this fact that it is not made with the precision and clearness with which the two former are. It declares, without qualification, that these continents have asserted and maintained their freedom and independence, and are no longer subject to colonization by any European power. This is not strictly accurate. Taken as a whole, these continents had not asserted and maintained their freedom and independence. At that period Great Britain had a larger portion of the continent in her possession than the United States. Russia had a considerable portion of it, and other powers possessed some portions on the southern parts of this continent. The declaration was broader than the fact, and exhibits precipitancy and want of due reflection. Besides there was an impropriety in it when viewed in conjunction with the foregoing declarations. I speak not in the language of censure. We were, as to them, acting in concert with England on a proposition coming from herself—a proposition of the utmost magnitude, and which we felt at the time to be essentially connected with our peace and safety; and of course it was due to propriety as well as policy that this declaration should be strictly in accordance with British feeling. Our power then was not what it is now, and we had to rely upon her co-operation to sustain the ground we had taken. We had then only about six or seven millions of people scattered and without such means of communication as we now possess to bring us together in a short period of time. The declaration accordingly, with respect to colonization, striking at England as well as Russia, gave offence to her, and that to such an extent that she refused to co-operate with us in settling the Russian question. Now, I will venture to say that if that declaration had come before that cautious cabinet—for Mr. Monroe was among the wisest and most cautious men I have ever known— it would have been modified and expressed with a far greater degree of precision and with much more delicacy in reference to the feelings of the British government."

The present international dispute is one full of encouragement and bright prospects for our country. The United States is the natural leader of the new world by force of its republican primacy, its wealth, population, and standing among the nations of the earth. The issues of the past, dividing North and South, are gone forever. The problems of the future may in no small degree involve the principles of the Monroe doctrine. "The question presented by the letters you have sent me," wrote Jefferson to Monroe in regard to the Canning-Rush documents, "is the most momentous which has ever been offered to my contemplation since that of Independence. That made us a nation; this sets our compass and points the course which we are to steer through the ocean of time opening on us."

It is not necessary here to dwell upon the successive assaults upon the rights of the people of Europe which were made by the Holy Alliance. The allies were Austria, Russia, Prussia, and England and France for a time. We now know that the crowned heads appealed only to the people, while they dreaded Napoleon, and after his fall they forgot their promises to their subjects, and preached but one discourse—the divine right of kings. In 1818, at Aix la Chapelle, they admitted France to the alliance. In 1820 they met at Trappee, in Moravia, did little and adjourned to meet again at Laybach in 1821. Here they began to show the mailed hand, and the next year, at the congress of Verona, the scheme was hatched to subvert the constitutional government of Spain, which later on was carried out. Then Naples, next Poland, and finally Hungary, were all crushed beneath this new juggernaut of kings. While the war on Spain was preparing, with France as the obsequious tool of the Holy Alliance, Russia began to turn lustful eye on the republics of South America. English rivalry in that quarter of the globe was the means of withdrawing Great Britain from the schemes of the allies, and led Mr. Canning to make overtures to Mr. Rush. Our minister at London acted nobly, and voiced the true sentiments of his countrymen, even before he could receive instructions from the State Department.

One startling fact should not be omitted here. It is surprising that none of the many prominent persons engaged in discussing the Monroe doctrine at the present time—neither the President nor his Secretary of State, neither Senator Lodge nor Mr. McMaster—has called attention to it. At the very hour that Mr. Monroe was consulting Jefferson respecting monarchical aggressions in South America, there was laid away in the Russian archives the record of a consultation held on the importance of reducing the South American republics under the dominion of Spain. It formed a part of that scheme that *the United States should be subjugated!* The memoir containing this startling proposal emanated in the year 1817 from the pen of Pozzo de Borgo—one of the most eminent of the remarkable corps of diplomatists by whom Russia has prepared the march of her armies. They do not impertinently volunteer their advice upon their government unasked. That memoir was therefore on a subject then under consideration by the Russian government, and its language gives the confirmation of history to the logic of Mr. Monroe's message. The principles of the Holy Alliance naturally led up to the necessity of their attempting to overthrow this republic as their crowning labor. Pozzo de Borgo rests his opinion on the incompatibility between our institutions and those of the allies. He says·

"Founded on the sovereignty of the people, the republic of the United States of America was a fire of which the daily contact with Europe threatened the latter with conflagration; that as an asylum for all innovators, it gave them the means of disseminating at a distance, by their writings and by the authority of their example, a poison of which the communication could not be questioned, as it was well known that the French Revolution had its origin in the United States; that already troublesome effects were felt from the presence of the French refugees in the United States."

He then proceeds to argue that our reduction would be an easy enterprise, while our augmenting power made us objects of fear to European monarchical governments.

Russia, therefore, had been meditating our subjugation, as a matter of sound policy, on the principle of the inherent incompatibility between our system and hers prior to the Spanish and Neapolitan revolutions, and before the congresses of Laybach and Verona had proclaimed her principles to the world, or elicited the warning protest of President Monroe. This important document of Pozzo de Borgo was brought to light by that profound statesman Senator Soulè in the year 1852.

An invitation was extended by Columbia and Mexico to the United States to attend the Congress of Panama in 1826, and take part in its deliberations. President Adams and his illustrious Secretary of State, Henry Clay, heartily approved of this congress, and took energetic measures to make it a success. If Mr. Lodge is really anxious to discover the author of the American system, let him turn from John Quincy Adams to Henry Clay. The great Kentuckian always favored a sort of Amphictyonic council of the free governments of the two Americas, as an offset to the Holy Alliance of the European monarchies. The Panama mission, which the administration so warmly espoused, never took effect, "though eventually sanctioned," says Thomas H. Benton, "by both houses of Congress." The President and Senate, always wrangling, did not intermit the pastime when this interesting question came up for discussion. The committee on Foreign Affairs reported adversely to the President's recommendations in favor of the mission. Littleton Waller Tazewell wrote the report, which was an able one, but it would have been a wiser one had it given sanction to the President's idea in all respects, except its moral or religious suggestion, which Senator Tazewell very properly rejected.*

When Russia and the Holy Allies crushed Hungary, the eloquent Kossuth came to these shores as the nation's guest. The famous exile had a memorable interview with Henry Clay. Age had softened the fire of "Harry of the West," who depicted the difficulties and futility of military operations by this country against Russia, and then added these parting words: "Thus, sir, after effecting nothing in such a war, after abandoning our ancient policy of amity and non-intervention in the affairs of other nations, and thus justifying them in abandoning the terms of forbearance and non-interference which

---

* The feeling in the Senate ran high against the President, whose message respecting an open or secret session on the Panama business was deemed offensive or intrusive. John Randolph, previously rather favorable to the mission, became incensed and assailed the President and Secretary of State, Mr. Clay, in such unmeasured terms of vituperation that a challenge from Clay followed, and resulted in the celebrated duel.

they have hitherto preserved towards us—after the downfall, perhaps, of the friends of liberal institutions in Europe—her despots, imitating and provoked by our fatal example, may turn upon us in our hour of weakness and exhaustion, and, with an almost irresistible force of reason and of arms, they may say to us: You have set us the example; you have quit your own to stand on foreign ground; you have abandoned the policy you professed in the day of your weakness, to interfere in the affairs of the people of this continent, in behalf of those principles, the supremacy of which you say is necessary to your prosperity, to your existence. We, in our turn, believing that your anarchical doctrines are destructive of, and that our monarchical principles are essential to the peace, security and happiness of our subjects, will obliterate the bed which has nourished such noxious weeds; we will crush you as the propagandists of doctrines so destructive to the peace and good order of the world. The indomitable spirit of our people might, and would be equal to the emergency, and we might remain unsubdued even by so tremendous a combination; but the consequences to us would be terrible enough."

It is a curious coincidence that Mr. Clay, the fiery and intrepid genius, whose warlike spirit made him joint leader on the floor of Congress with the equally bold and patriotic Calhoun in our second war with England, should stand forth in his old age, as did Mr. Calhoun in his last days, the eloquent advocate of non-intervention, the champion of those principles which received their deepest and most earnest expression in the farewell address of George Washington.

The message of Mr. Buchanan in 1860 was in the strict line of American precedents in relation to the Monroe doctrine. At that period France, England and Spain were threatening an armed intervention in Mexico. General Cass, then Secretary of State, entered a vigorous protest, and President Buchanan, in his annual message to Congress (December, 1860), used the following language: "I deemed it my duty to recommend to Congress in my last annual message, the employment of a sufficient military force to penetrate into the interior. . . . European governments would have been deprived of all pretext to interfere in the territorial and domestic concerns of Mexico. We should thus have been relieved from the obligation of resisting, even by force, should this become necessary, any attempt by these governments to deprive our neighboring republic of portions of her territory—a duty from which we could not shrink without abandoning the traditional and established policy of the American people."

Soon afterwards our beloved country was plunged into domestic war between the States, and Napoleon the Third took advantage of our misfortunes to set up a monarchy in Mexico. In a few years more the United States government was again in a position to make its will-known, and to enforce respect for its traditional policy. The fate of the Emperor Maximilian furnished an impressive warning to Europe of the inexorable purpose of this republic to carry out the Monroe doctrine at all hazards. This digest of precedents we deem quite sufficient as a solemn protest against any departure, at this day, from the formal and indestructible declaration of American principles uttered by James Monroe in 1823.

www.ingramcontent.com/pod-product-compliance
Lightning Source LLC
Chambersburg PA
CBHW031744230426
43669CB00007B/481